ROAD to Fatherhood

ROAD
to Fatherhood

How to Help Young Dads
Become Loving
and Responsible Parents

Jon Morris

Morning
Glory
Press

Buena Park, California

Library of Congress Cataloging-in-Publication Data
Morris, Jon, 1972-
    ROAD to fatherhood: how to help young dads become loving and
responsible parents / Jon Morris
        p. cm.
Includes bibliographical references and index.
ISBN 1-885356-91-9 (hc.) -- ISBN 1-885356-92-7 (pbk.)
    I. Reaching Out to Adolescent Dads (Program) 2. Teenage fathers--
Services for -- Virginia -- Roanoke. 3. Teenage fathers--Virginia--
Roanoke--Case studies. I. Title.

HZ756.7 .M67 2002
306.874'2--dc21   2001059072

MORNING GLORY PRESS, INC.
6595 San Haroldo Way   Buena Park, CA 90620-3748
714.828.1998   1.888.612.8254
e-mail info@morningglorypress.com
Web site www.morningglorypress.com
Printed and bound in the United States of America

CONTENTS

• Interviewing applicants
• Organizational ability a must • Filing information
• Educating yourself and your staff

PREFACE

I couldn't have been at my new job at the Health Department as the coordinator of the For Males Only program for more than three months when I heard a statement from a young man that pushed me into the fatherhood movement. We were in the cafeteria at a local high school talking to a group of sophomores, juniors, and seniors about safer sex. My colleague and I had some great dialogue going with our participants when the subject changed to fatherhood.

"What are you supposed to do if you already have kids?" the young man asked.

We started explaining to him that you can still be safe by using condoms or abstaining from having sex when another participant asked the young dad, "You taking care of your child?"

"Yeah, I take care of my kid," the young father replied.

I asked him how difficult it was.

"It ain't hard at all," he replied. "I give my baby's momma a check every week. I handle my business."

To a lot of young men, being a good father is giving his child's mother some money every now and then. Yet we wonder why they think simply giving money makes them a good dad.

The answer is simple. Many teenage fathers grew up in a single parent home in which mom was the custodial parent. Their father may or may not have given money. If their father gave them money and they had a good relationship with him, then they may think that their father was a pretty good dad. If their father did not pay child support, and they are paying, then they are already doing more than their own father did. They must be doing something right.

Some people give a young dad the impression that paying child support is *all* that is required to raise a child. Parents, teachers, clergy urge the young father, "Get a job so you can support your child." The perception is ingrained in America's brain that fathers must be financial providers or they are not good fathers. For that matter, they are less of a man if they can't hold down a *good* job.

Financial support is a crucial part of parenting, but fathers are even more important to their children as role models, caregivers, someone their children can depend on. We need to help young fathers with workforce preparation, but we also need support programs for young fathers to help them become *involved* and caring parents of their children.

This book offers guidance for developing a program designed to help young fathers not only support their children financially, but also learn the art and skills of parenting. Most of all, a young fathers program can help young men meet the challenge of being truly involved parents, no matter what their relationship may be with their child's other parent. With such a program, you *can* make a difference, an important difference, in their lives and in their children's lives.

Jon Morris
February, 2002

FOREWORD

There are many things that go through a young man's mind when he learns for the first time that he is going to be a father. Most people, however, don't want to acknowledge the fact that young men can be as complex in their thoughts and feelings as young women can. Fear, anxiety, apathy, and joy are some of the emotions that young men feel when they hear about the life altering news. That is why I felt compelled to write the foreword to this important book.

There are different stages of fatherhood. Anger, grief, bargaining, denial, and finally acceptance are true emotions that fall upon men of all age, race, and socioeconomic status. The emotions are ever changing. I know this because I have felt some of these emotions myself.

"I feel like a woman who has been raped and doesn't believe in abortion." That is a line from my play called, "What's on the Hearts of Men." When a young man gets a girl pregnant, he has no say in what she does with her body; therefore, he has no decision in the process of whether she will have the baby. Boo, the young father-to-be in the play, is upset because he doesn't want a baby yet. He wanted to get married first and establish a life for himself and his fiancée before they started their family. He feels trapped, betrayed. Many young men have these same feelings when they learn they will soon be a father.

Some say, "The young man should have thought about that before he lay down with her." I won't argue that, but we all know in the real world, everything doesn't go smoothly or as planned.

The journey of becoming a father and even becoming a man is a difficult one for a lot of dads. I've spent a lot of money and time in the Family Court System in New York fighting for the right to be more involved in my child's life. Many young men don't have the opportunity to go to court or to be represented by a lawyer, and they are left on the outside looking in. He has no say in how his child is raised, and all he is told to do is pay child support.

The bottom line is as men, if we make a baby, we must be involved, and that includes all the good and the bad and all the emotions that are attached. At the end of the day when it is all said and done, we are still fathers, and we must be men to be fathers. It's not an easy job, but it is the most rewarding thing we will ever do. That is why your job, as you work with young fathers, is so important. Many of the young men that you will reach will not know how to acknowledge or express their emotions.

You must have their trust, and you must be willing to stand in the gap for them. We can't expect young dads to be willing to "just go to work and support your children" when they may not have those skills. You must also teach them to get in touch with their feelings so they can be emotionally involved in their child's life. Nobody wants to pay for a car they can't drive, and no father wants simply to pay child support without experiencing the joys of being a dad.

I also urge you to work with whomever you can to support your program. Obtaining public and corporate support is difficult for fatherhood programs. Many see dads as interchangeable parts to the puzzle. Some feel mentors can replace them, but kids *need* their fathers.

What the ROAD program in Roanoke, Virginia, has done is remarkable. The Roanoke community is no different from yours. Crime, poverty, domestic violence, and drugs are as prevalent in Roanoke, Virginia, as they are in every community in this country. The ROAD program has been around for more than six years. They did it without funding from the state or local foundations. They have succeeded because they felt a desire to help young men and their families, particularly their children. Their staff works hard and will continue to work hard to provide hope for the dads that come to their program.

It may not be popular to work with young men and fathers. I guarantee you, however, it could be the most important work that you ever do.

It is up to you to help these young fathers express themselves so they can be good, supportive fathers for their children and good men and husbands for their families.

Malik Yoba

Malik Yoba is the creator and executive producer of the multimedia production, "The Great American Father's Day Celebration" and playwright and director of the musical, "What's on the Hearts of Men."

ROAD Pledge

I am a FATHER . . . no matter what my age may be.

I am a FATHER . . . I will always put my child's interests before my own.

I am a FATHER . . . I will not turn my back on my responsibility.

I am a FATHER . . . I will work hard to provide financially for my child.

I am a FATHER . . . I will respect the mother of my child.

I am a FATHER . . . I will be there emotionally for my child.

I am a FATHER . . . I know there is no greater gift than a child.

I am a FATHER . . . I know there is no greater responsibility, no greater joy, no greater honor than being a DAD!

ACKNOWLEDGMENTS

First of all, I thank God. You have blessed me tremendously as well as our program. All praise and honor go to You. I thank my wonderful wife, Katrina, for allowing me to venture into the computer room in the evenings to write this book, as well as supporting me and my career, and understanding the crazy hours I sometimes work. I thank my stepson, Ameer, for just being a good boy and a great big brother, and my active daughter, Nina. They all make everyday life better.

I thank my mother, Carol, for being there when our father was not. She is the epitome of strength, courage, and what a real parent should be. She always sacrificed for her children, and for that, I can never repay her. Also, thanks to my wonderful sisters, Angie and Melanie, and our late brother Michael, for always showing love, support, and the true meaning of family.

I also thank Anthony Drakeford. He laid the foundation of the For Males Only program and gave me the confidence and support to pursue this career.

A big thank you goes to my former supervisor, Donna Proctor. She read every line of this book (made many corrections) and gave me advice on how to make it better. She has always been one of our biggest supporters. I recognize all the staff at the Roanoke City Health Department for being so supportive of our work and being true public health professionals.

Craig McMillan, coordinator of the Fatherhood, Manhood, and

16

           Acknowledgments

Empowerment Program in Virginia Beach, is a good friend and a great
role model for the young men with whom he works. Thanks for everything, Mac! And to Fred Watson, the father of male oriented programs in
Virginia. Thank you for your wisdom and inspiration.

I also thank Alfred Dowe, Jr., Deacon Gaither, Deacon Stovall,
Anthony Cummings, and my pastor, Rev. Adrian Dowell, the men's
fellowship, and all the members of Shiloh Baptist Church.

I want to acknowledge the greatest staff in the world. I thank Joni
Plantinga for being so great at working with the young fathers and
mothers. Also to Lee Pusha, my calming influence, I thank God for you.
Correlli Rasheed, a true fatherhood pioneer, is a great addition to this
program. My new boss, Rosana Anderson, and everyone at TAP, thank
you for welcoming us. To Felicia White, our child support case manager,
I'm so glad you are part of our team.

I have to say thank you to Lorin Harris, Dr. Jeff Johnson, Pam
Wilson, Uriel Johnson, Byron Browder, Ed Ridgeway, Mark Elliot, Dee
Wallace, Herb Turner, and everyone involved in the Fathers at Work
project at the Mott Foundation, Public/Private Ventures, and NPCL. Also
to my friends at STRIVE in Chicago, Rubicon in Richmond, CA, CEO
and VFI in New York, and Impact Services in Philadelphia, thank you
for your support, expertise, and professionalism. Working with you all
has truly been a blessing to me.

I also thank Ferrum College and Dean David Newcombe. You always
treated me like an adult, even though I didn't always act like one. I can't
leave out Giles High School and my four mentors, Allen McGraw, Frank
Cahoon, Coach Rusty Kelly, and Coach Steve Ragsdale. All are great
men who had a tremendous impact on my life. And my man, J. R.
Coleman, thanks for everything. I also say thank you to Malik Yoba for
his help and the great work that he does.

I want to say thank you to the wonderful staff at Morning Glory Press
for their patience, professionalism, and incredible insight. Carole and
Karen have been wonderful to me. And to Jeanne and her husband Bob,
you guys are wonderful. Thank you all for this tremendous experience.

Last but not least, I thank Ron J. Clark, director of the Virginia
Fatherhood Campaign. He has taught me so much, not just about
fatherhood, but about God and life as well. He truly loves his family and
his job, and he taught me never to put my job before my family. He
continues to be a powerful influence and mentor to me.

If I forgot anyone, please forgive me, as it was a mistake of the mind,
and not of the heart.

Jon Morris

To young fathers everywhere
and to my brother Michael

Many teen fathers need help
in becoming responsible, loving, and mature parents.

INTRODUCTION

The adolescent male is one of the most complex creatures walking the earth today. He is too young to be a man, yet too old to be a kid. The adolescent male is expected to be responsible and mature, but in many cases, he is still "mama's baby boy." Adolescence is supposed to be a time when a young man seeks his independence and creates his new identity. He is expected to acquire the tools and knowledge that a teenage boy must possess when he enters the world of manhood.

Many young males are being raised in a female-headed household. It is becoming more common that a single parent is raising children, and most of the time, that parent is the mother. As a result, many adolescent males do not have good role models and are not being taught how to become a man.

When a father is absent, a child is more likely to use drugs, suffer depression, and have poor school performance and lower self-esteem. Children from father-absent families are at an increased risk for living in poverty and committing crimes . . . and the list goes on, according to Wade F. Horn (2002: *Father Facts*, National Fatherhood Initiative). When a father is not there to provide, care for, and discipline, it makes it difficult for the mother to enforce rules, instill values, and monitor her children's activities.

Another statistic linked to father absence is increased sexual activity. Young people are having sex at a younger age. Teenage girls are 150 percent more likely to engage in sexual activity if a father is not present *(Father Facts)*. If teenage girls are having sex earlier, they are putting themselves at risk of cervical cancer, sexually transmitted infections, and, of course, having a baby.

Many teen pregnancy prevention efforts are targeted toward girls. After all, they are the ones that get pregnant. After the baby is born, the teenage mothers get most of the attention, and this makes sense because they give birth. They carry the baby for nine months so the bulk of the services needs to be directed toward them.

What about the fathers? While in many teenage pregnancies, the baby is fathered by an older male, there are also many teenage dads, and these young fathers need help.

High Expectations for Teen Dads

When an adolescent male becomes a father, he is expected to become a man automatically. He is expected to provide, be there for the mother, and help raise and nurture his newborn child. Is this realistic? One day the young male is out playing basketball with his friends, hanging out at the mall, doing what teenagers do. Then he is expected to become a man overnight. There are thirty-year-old men who are not that responsible.

We need to help young fathers and provide services for them because many others are betting against them. Many courtrooms are biased against fathers, especially teenage fathers. Most social service organizations are predominately staffed by women, some of whom are very cold toward teen dads. Many maternal grandparents are keeping these young fathers away from their children. "You did this to my daughter and now you can't see her," is their sentiment. Sometimes maternal grandparents do more harm than good.

Teenage fathers need guidance, support, encouragement, love, resources, employment, education, legal advice, patience, and much, much more. Workforce preparation, assistance with job hunting, employment, and parenting education are all top priority.

Young men need to know about STIs (Sexually Transmitted Infections), how to protect themselves and their partners from contracting STIs, and how to prevent pregnancy.

In fact, they need assistance with services they don't even know exist. They need legal help so they won't be abused by the system. They need advocates so DSS (Department of Social Services) and other organizations won't disrespect them or deny them services. They also need help in communicating with maternal grandparents and even their own parents.

Support groups need to be established to help teenage fathers become men. They need a support group so they can be in an environment that is not threatening, and so other fathers can mentor them and provide positive peer pressure. Older fathers can share experiences and give insight to the young dads, and young fathers can gain a sense of what a real dad is supposed to be like. They can also use the support group to celebrate their successes. This is important because no one else may notice, and they may feel that all they are working for is in vain.

Teachers, coaches, educators, and society in general need to start helping the dads. If support is not given to the teenage father, he may not ever become involved in raising his child. And the absent-father cycle continues.

The biggest reason we need to provide programs for teenage fathers is for their children. Kids deserve to have two parents who get along, who work for a better life for them, and who love them unconditionally. Children need their dads, because dads are supposed to keep them safe, provide for them, and provide emotional support that they can't get anywhere else.

Teen Dads and School Programs

If you're teaching a daily parenting class for teen parents in high school or junior high, are you including teen fathers? When schools started offering special classes for teen parents, the parents were almost entirely mothers. Common names for these programs were School Age Mothers (SAM) and Teen Mother Program (TMP). Now program titles tend to be less sexist, as in Teenage Parent Program (TAPP). Fathers, however, are non-existent in some of these classes/programs, and in others, a distinct minority. GRADS (Graduation, Reality, and Dual-role Skills) programs in Ohio and other states have emphasized the needs of both parents and, as a consequence, about twelve percent of their students are fathers.

This book focuses on the needs of the fathers. Teen fathers who have not graduated from high school certainly need to be in school or in a GED (General Educational Development) program. They also have many additional needs, and suggestions for meeting some of these needs are offered.

If you are already teaching teen dads in a school program, you're making a real difference in their lives. This book will help you either expand your services to them or show you how to collaborate with other services to develop a truly comprehensive program for teen fathers. A weekly support group for fathers plus job skills and career development may be needed.

Recruiting teen fathers into a school teen parent program may take extra effort. If most of the fathers of your students' babies are not on campus, the need for developing out-of-school services is even greater. And don't forget that there will be other teen fathers on your campus, fathers whose children and their mothers are not enrolled at your school. These fathers need your support, too.

ROAD, the Early Years

The ROAD program is a component of the Fatherhood and Families program at Total Action Against Poverty (TAP) in Roanoke, Virginia. The ROAD and For Males Only (FMO) programs, formerly with the Roanoke (Virginia) City Health Department, joined TAP in July 2001 in order to expand services to young fathers. Part of that expansion is the Fathers at Work program which serves non-custodial fathers 30 years of age and under. Fathers at Work is a national demonstration project funded by the Charles Stewart Mott Foundation.

FMO is a teenage prevention program which targets young males, ages 10 – 19. The FMO program started operating on a part-time basis in 1989, and was coordinated by Anthony Drakeford (who is still employed with the program as the health educator) from 1990 - 1995. A grant allowed the FMO program to expand and add a full-time coordinator. Anthony already had a full-time job, and I became the program's first full-time coordinator in June, 1995.

FMO aggressively performed educational sessions throughout the city. We conducted programs in juvenile correctional facilities, summer camps, schools, churches, playgrounds, and housing developments. During the first quarter of 1995, we exceeded the number of participants in the program's previous year by 400 percent.

We were often asked, "What about the fathers?" We couldn't answer that question for the young fathers because we were not working with them. In fact, during many of these meetings, Anthony and I heard nothing but negative comments toward young fathers and young men in general. One educator even said, "Teenage pregnancy is the result of irresponsible young men," as if females had no part in it.

After some brainstorming, Anthony and I decided to start a teen fathers program. We needed a catchy name, an acronym that people would remember. After much debate and discussion, we came up with Reaching Out to Adolescent Dads (ROAD). We were ready to begin the most successful teen father program in the country. However, getting started was far harder than we expected.

At First, Few Dads Came

We called the local teen mother programs and told them of our wonderful idea. They were as excited as we were. They gave us names of young fathers to contact. We had ten names on our initial list. We made phone calls to all ten fathers, and all ten fathers said they would attend the first meeting.

Three young men showed up. We were floored by the low attendance. We could not believe that the guys weren't as anxious as we were to participate in the ROAD program.

"Three fathers, and everyone said they'd be here," I said to Anthony. I was depressed that not all ten fathers showed up. It reflected in our presentation that night, and this was one of the worst programs we had ever conducted.

The next week we had four young men show up. This sounds great, right? An increase in numbers is always a good thing. However, only one young father from the previous week was in attendance, along with three new young men. The only reason we had these three guys there was because their probation officer had accompanied them to the meeting and told them they had to stay. They didn't want to be there.

Once again, the evening program was terrible. We tried to answer questions and talk about things fathers should know. However, we had not done our homework or educated ourselves first.

The lowest point of that first group of fathers came during the third week. We invited a lawyer to come and speak to the fathers to discuss their paternal rights. No one showed up although six of the fathers had promised they'd be there.

I was extremely embarrassed and apologized to the lawyer for the absence of our group. He appeared to understand and told us, "Don't worry about it, you know how young men can be at times. We can reschedule and do it again." This made me feel better at the time, but he was obviously upset that we had wasted his time. To this day, he will not return my phone calls.

Over the next six months we tried to enroll and help fathers with little success. Support group meetings weren't much better. We just couldn't reach the dads. By June, 1996, we had zero fathers enrolled in the ROAD program. ZERO! We had failed miserably, and thought about throwing in the towel. Besides, we were getting paid to conduct FMO programs, not ROAD programs. We were doing that in addition to our FMO responsibilities.

But because we thought it was a needed program, and because of my competitiveness, we decided to give it another chance. We looked at what wasn't working, rolled up our sleeves, and pushed harder.

I started to educate myself on other teen father programs (there were not too many at the time). I read books, made phone calls, and surfed the Internet. After we educated ourselves and gained more insight, our program attracted some participants. It was hard work recruiting each young father, but it was worth it. I have worked for more than seven years with adolescent males, and provided services to teen dads for six years. Today we have about 30 clients at a time, with a yearly total of about 150.

Strategies for Starting a Program

This book is a result of our early struggles in the ROAD program. Here you'll find suggestions and strategies for starting and implementing a teen father program, strategies which we hope will help you get your program going more quickly than we did. Some of the suggestions appear to be simply common sense. However, ROAD did not follow some of these strategies in the beginning, and we suffered tremendously.

Included here are stories of teenage fathers and the challenges each one faces being a new dad. Each story has a father facing a different issue common among young fathers, followed by strategies designed to help that individual father succeed. The events depicted here are struggles that teen fathers have faced; they are real.

Most teenage fathers, of course, are plagued with more than one challenging issue. These suggestions are starting points, and some teenage fathers will need still different approaches because no method is right for everyone. These are strategies that the ROAD program has tried, with some success.

Many teen fathers described here no longer have a relationship with the mother. This is not meant to portray some stereotype. The fathers in our program who do have a loving relationship with their child's mother tend to be less stressed than those without such a relationship.

Part of our job with the ROAD program is to have the mother and father of the child form a communicating, respectful relationship. Many teen mothers with whom we have dealt have been helpful and positive.

Following the chapters containing stories of teen fathers are several chapters with specific information designed to help you develop your program for teen fathers. Planning is basic, and tips and techniques are offered for this important phase. Hiring your staff is discussed, as is choosing and evaluating curriculum. The hard work of finding and recruiting young fathers is stressed, and strategies are offered for organizing for case management.

The Appendix includes an annotated bibliography of relevant resources, a list of places to contact for further help, a variety of forms we use in the ROAD program (and which you are welcome to copy and use), and some passages written by members of the ROAD program. Their perspective is included because they are the reason we entered this fascinating field.

Perhaps the most important truth we learned from our early days: You can't do anything about the people who are absent (except through outreach and follow-up). The ones who sit in front of you are there because they need YOU! If only three fathers show up, you may feel your program is a failure, or you may think you are the one that failed. Don't believe it. Give everything you have to however many you have in your group. It's a lot easier to start with three than with zero.

Positive Change Happens

A young father, D.C. Dunnaville, entered our program in late fall, 1998. He was unemployed, behind on his child support payments, and had not seen his child in about a month. He wanted help with finding a job, and he had many questions about child support. He was referred to our program by a local teen mother group, a bit unusual for us because we don't get many referrals from programs for teenage mothers. (Many of my colleagues across the country share the same struggle of obtaining referrals from programs that assist young mothers.)

D.C. began attending support groups, but was a withdrawn member. He was friendly to all the participants and got along well with the other fathers, but he just didn't get involved in the discussion. One night after one of our father's meetings, I pulled

D.C. to the side and asked him why he didn't speak up in group. "All these guys in the room are trying to do something for their kids. They're trying to be the best dad they can be. I'm not. I haven't seen my son for about two months, and I haven't even tried. I'd feel like a hypocrite if I spoke up during the meeting."

It took courage for him to be honest with me. Because he was truthful with me, we were able to start an honest dialogue about his dreams and wishes for his son. D.C. and I began to talk about the struggles he was facing with the child's mother and the difficulty he had finding a job.

He told me that his son was better off without him at that point. I didn't agree with his statement, but I had to honor the steps he was taking toward progress. A young dad needs to be ready to improve his situation. It doesn't matter how badly I want it, he has to *want* to improve.

In the spring of 1999, D.C. called me and said he was going into the army. This caught me completely off guard. He was making some progress and I thought we were close to a break-through, but he felt this would be the best thing for him and his son. I admired him for thinking about his son in regard to this life-altering decision.

Two months after he entered the Army, D.C. was medically discharged. He was a little despondent about his fate with the Army, but he called me and came back to the program. He was soon hired at a packaging plant and once again began attending support group meetings. He started taking his son to Head Start in the morning before he went to work. A little later, he began to pick his son up to take him home for a visit. He then graduated to having his son spend the night. The young father kept improving his situation through employment, custody agreement, living situation, etc.

Today, D.C. serves as a mentor to the young dads enrolled in the ROAD program. He has his own apartment and has custody of his son. He has worked the same job for almost two years. He is a prime example of what can happen with positive guidance and assistance from a young father program.

The ROAD program, of course, doesn't take all the credit.

D.C. had to *want* to improve his situation. However, he probably would not otherwise have gotten the services that he needed such as legal help, employment information, and educational assistance. He wouldn't have had the opportunity to speak with other dads like him about the struggles associated with being a young father.

Providing a teen father program is not easy. When I began my research before starting ROAD, there was very little information concerning teen father programs, which made our job even harder. Materials on where to begin, services to provide, and evaluation procedures were difficult to obtain.

This book can make your job a little easier.

1

Tony — Whenever He Messes Up, Momma Helps Him Out

Tony's mother is furious.

"What do you mean, you're going to be a father?" she asked.

Tony sat on the sofa looking at the floor, wishing he were any place but here.

"You can't even keep your room clean," she continued. "How on earth can you raise a child?"

"I'll get a job," he said. As soon as the words came out of his mouth, he could feel it coming.

"You're fifteen years old. Nobody is going to hire a fifteen-year-old boy," she said.

Tony felt a fear in his heart that he had never known before. A tear fell down his cheek, followed by another. He then felt his mother's arms around him as she said, "Don't worry, baby, we'll work it out. We'll figure something out."

This is what Tony was waiting to hear. Just like it has always been. Whenever he messes up, Mama is there to help him. It's not Tony's fault he has grown up like this, and it may not even be his mother's fault. Tony's father has been out of the house for ten years now. Tony vaguely remembers him. His dad never sends a birthday card, Christmas present, or even picks up the phone to see how Tony is doing. Tony hates his father.

Tony's mother didn't want her only son, her youngest child, to hurt like his sisters did. They were older, and they remember how badly their dad treated their mother. So Mom sheltered Tony and started doing everything for him. She cleaned his room, did his laundry, and even stood up for him when he got in trouble at school.

As he was growing up, whenever Tony wanted anything, his mother would oblige him and see that he got that baseball bat or the toy he was eyeing. Tony didn't see the harm in this. As a matter of fact, it was normal to him.

As Tony lay in bed, trying to think about anything other than the fact that he was going to be a dad, his mind wandered to Ginny. He wondered what she was feeling right now, what her parents had said to her. In the back of his mind, he also thought about the impact this would have on his social life and his chance to date other girls. Tony didn't love Ginny, and he didn't think that she loved him. After all, it was just a "hook-up."

"Hey Ginny," he remembered telling her, "why don't you come to my house after school and we can study for that algebra test?" Ginny had always been attracted to him and he knew this.

"Sure," she said without hesitation. "I'll meet you there, say 4:00." Tony was excited. His sisters weren't going to be there and his mom was working until 7 o'clock.

"Do you have protection?" she asked.

"Naw," Tony said. "Don't worry, I'll pull out in time." Tony lay in bed looking toward the ceiling wondering how he got her pregnant. He did pull out in time, or so he thought. And besides, she was on the pill. She wasn't supposed to get pregnant in the first place.

"She probably didn't even take the pill," Tony said bitterly to himself. She should have to pay for this child, since she obviously messed up. Tony still could not sleep. He thought of how his life used to be and how it would change. He loved going to the movies, playing Sony Playstation, eating pizza, and just hanging out with the fellas. Now all he could picture was changing diapers and working to provide for his child.

One Year Later

"Son, do you have a job?" the judge asked.

"No sir, not yet," replied Tony. It was still like a dream to him standing in that courtroom. How could she bring him to court? Besides, his mother already bought Pampers, formula, and clothes for the baby. Isn't that enough?

"When was the last time you saw your daughter?" the judge asked.

"About a week ago."

Before he even finished his sentence, Ginny blurted out, "Huh, more like two months ago."

Who was this girl? This wasn't the same girl who came to his house with him after school that day. This wasn't the same girl who flirted with him every day in algebra class. This girl was mean. How could she bring him to court?

The judge was getting frustrated with him by now. "You just don't get it, do you, young man? You are not a kid anymore. You lost that privilege when you decided you were man enough to have sex." The judge was now speaking in a military-like tone. "You better get a job and fast. I'm ordering you to pay $30 per week."

Thirty dollars a week? Was he crazy? Tony started thinking of everything he could buy with $120 per month. Shoes, clothes, CDs, video games. The judge started speaking again and snapped him out of his daydream.

"Mr. Jennings, I also suggest that you get to know your little girl. She deserves to know both her parents. I don't care how young they are. I don't want to see you back in this courtroom because you haven't been paying that child support. Do we understand each other?"

"Yes, sir," Tony replied, almost sarcastically.

As Tony walked out of the courtroom with his mother, she put her arm around his shoulder, and said, "Don't worry, baby. We'll figure something out."

Possible Approaches

Working with young fathers like Tony is extremely difficult. As an educator or outreach worker, you are competing against a lifetime of pampering and spoiling. As a matter of fact, his mother continues to spoil him. Tony is simply immature – too young to understand the full impact of the responsibilities that being a father, a good father, bring. Getting a father like Tony to enroll in your program may be difficult. He doesn't comprehend the seriousness of the situation. However, he is young, only sixteen, and that could work to his benefit. Younger males are sometimes easier to influence than someone twenty years old. Or, in some cases, they may be harder to change because of their immaturity.

The first step is to make a connection with him and his mother. If you sell his mother on the program, you'll probably sell Tony on the idea as well. This may take letters, phone calls, and late night home visits to accommodate the mother's work schedule. You might also participate in activities that he enjoys like playing basketball or video games. This will help Tony see you as a real person, and not someone who is there to make his life miserable.

Job Search Assistance

The second step is to help him find a job. Don't do it for him. This is what his mother has been doing his whole life. Teach him how to fill out applications. Coach him about his dress and how to approach a manager at the establishment where he is seeking employment. Conduct practice interviews with him. This will get him used to the questions that his future boss will ask him. If necessary, give him a ride to pick up applications and go to interviews.

Involve him in support group meetings. Tony needs to see other guys like him going through the same things. He can relate to his peers. They will have a big impact on him, maybe even more than you will. At the support group meetings, be sure to cover pregnancy and disease prevention and contraception. Tony probably doesn't want to have another child soon.

Education, Parenting

Take Tony to see his baby. Supervised visits will give him confidence and support. Show him how to hold the baby or ask the mother to show him. It is often a scary situation for a young dad to visit his child at the mother's home. His child's maternal grandparents probably already dislike him. He doesn't get along with his baby's mother, and she probably criticizes every move he makes.

Encourage him to enroll in a parenting class. If he is paying $120 per month, he certainly will want to have some of the joy of being an involved father. If he's still in school, is there a teen parent class there that he could join? If not, check on Parents as Teachers or other parenting programs in your community, preferably one that is designed for very young parents.

It's important that you promote education and encourage his involvement in school. Many young men feel they must drop out of school and get a full-time job in order to pay child support. This is not a viable solution to his problem. It is nearly impossible to be a good provider without an education. If his mind is set on full-time employment, encourage him to obtain his GED (General Education Development) and enter a job training program. Some school districts will not allow a student to get a GED unless they've been absent from school for a year or more. Educate yourself and your staff on the requirements for GED classes in your area.

The most important thing to keep in mind is to stay with Tony as much as possible. Give him as much support and keep in contact with him as often as you can. The younger a father is, the easier it is to get off track.

Once he shows that he is taking on more responsibility, give him more. Step back just enough that you can still catch him if he falls, but give him a chance to walk on his own. An example would be for Tony to petition for visitation. If Tony demonstrates willingness to be in his daughter's life and the responsibility to care for her, encourage him to take this step.

She loves being with her dad.

2

Isaiah — Hard Worker But No Diploma, No Promotion

Isaiah woke up early today. It was normally his day off from Dandridge Distributing Corporation, and he would sleep until noon. When the alarm awoke him at 7 a.m., he jumped out of bed like it was Christmas morning. Today was not like any other day off. He had an interview at 9:00 with the plant manager at Dandridge Distributing, or DDC as the people who worked there called it.

Isaiah had been with DDC for two years. He was hired about two weeks before his daughter was born. He didn't think he had a chance for the job then, but he applied anyway because he knew he had to provide for his daughter. He was hired as a production worker, packing trucks with the auto parts that DDC distributed to stores around the state. It was a great job, even though it was hard work. He loved the fact that he was making real money at $8.25 per hour. He knew he didn't want to work fast-food making minimum wage.

Isaiah worked hard at his job. He always showed up at 6:45, and was hard at work when most of the other guys were sprinting to the time clock so they wouldn't be late. He usually clocked out at 3 p.m., but often volunteered to stay late if they were behind in getting the trucks loaded. The supervisors loved him because he never complained. The only time he would call in to miss work was if his daughter, Jessica, was sick or needed to see the doctor.

He also loved his job because he was able to pick Jessica up from the babysitter every afternoon and spend a couple of hours with her before he took her home. Natasha, Jessica's mother, liked the fact that Isaiah paid child support without fail, and even provided Jessica with clothes, diapers, formula, and toys.

Isaiah made enough money to help his mother with the bills and groceries. She wouldn't take rent from her son, because she said as long as she has a roof over her head, so does Isaiah. His mom appreciated the help with the phone, cable, and power bills. It was a perfect job, and it was about to get better.

A new position was opening up. Ted, the current supervisor, was leaving the company. He told Isaiah that he'd put in a good word for him. Isaiah applied for the position and hoped he had a chance.

"Isaiah, come on in," said Mr. Franklin, the plant manager. As Isaiah walked through the door, he gave Mr. Franklin a firm handshake, making sure it wasn't too flimsy.

"Thank you, sir," said Isaiah. They were in the interview for about 30 minutes talking about the job duties, requirements, and responsibilities that came with the position.

The job Isaiah was hoping to get was floor supervisor. The floor supervisor didn't help load the truck like Isaiah had been doing for the last two years. He would be in charge of making sure the other guys loaded the truck properly, efficiently, and with the correct shipment. He would even get paid more money, $10.05 per hour. It also made him feel good to be considered for this promotion because most of the men and women that worked with him were older than he was.

"Everything looks good, Isaiah," said Mr. Franklin. "Every-one speaks highly of you, and I think you'll make a great floor supervisor as long as your application comes out okay. We could let you know something by the end of the week."

Isaiah felt great. "Thank you, Mr. Franklin," he said. "I know I can do the job." The two shook hands one more time and Isaiah went home feeling better than he had ever felt (except for the first time he held his daughter).

He felt so good, he went straight from the interview to pick Jessica up from the sitter's, and spent the day buying his daughter new shoes and ice cream. Isaiah loved his daughter more than anything in the world. He used to love Natasha. They had dated for six months, but they were quite different people. They didn't realize how far apart they were until Jessica was on the way.

Natasha loved school and Isaiah was the total opposite. She was going to college and Isaiah knew he would never step one foot into a college classroom. After Jessica was born, they agreed to go their separate ways, but they still had a good relationship. She was polite to him and let him know about all the things a dad should know about his daughter. They were friends, he thought, although they never did anything together or talked about anything other than their daughter.

The next morning Isaiah showed up at work at his customary time of 6:45. He worked extra hard that morning, just in case the supervisors were checking him out. He was about to go on break when his floor supervisor came to him and said, "Isaiah, Mr. Franklin wants to see you in his office."

"This is it," Isaiah thought to himself. "They're going to offer me the job."

Isaiah knocked on Mr. Franklin's office door.

"Come in."

"You wanted to see me, Mr. Franklin?" Isaiah asked.

"Yes, Isaiah, have a seat." Mr. Franklin didn't seem to be in a very good mood. "Isaiah, we seem to have a problem with your application."

"What problem?" Isaiah asked.

"We did some checking on your application, a routine check that we do when we hire supervisors and managers. In your application you checked that you had a high school diploma. Yet, it seems that you never graduated from high school. Is that correct?"

Isaiah had a lump in his throat and an empty feeling in his stomach. "Uh, not exactly, Mr. Franklin."

Mr. Franklin stared at him and asked, "Then why did you put it on your application?"

Isaiah looked for an answer. "Well, I plan on going back to get my diploma."

That wasn't the truth. What he felt like saying was, "Because I hated school."

The silence in the room was unbearable. Mr. Franklin was writing something on what appeared to be his application. After what seemed to be an eternity, Mr. Franklin finally said something.

"I'm sorry, Isaiah, but we can't hire you for the position. As a matter of fact, we are going to have to let you go altogether."

"What?" Isaiah asked in disbelief. "I'm being fired for not getting my diploma? I've been here for two years, worked my butt off every day, and you're firing me?"

"I'm sorry, son," Mr. Franklin said. "You lied on your application, and it is our policy that we hire only high school graduates or someone with a GED. Do you have a GED?"

"No, I don't," he said. He was starting to get angry, and he did all he could not to storm out of the office. He couldn't believe this was happening. "I've been here for two years. I've gotten great evaluations, never called in sick except for when I had to take care of my daughter, and always volunteer for overtime. It's not fair to lose my job now."

"I'm sorry, son, but my hands are tied. You lied on your application. There is nothing I can do. I really wish I could."

So that was it. Nothing left to say. He didn't want to get on his hands and knees and beg. He had too much pride for that.

Isaiah walked out of the office without saying a word. He felt numb. He clocked out and walked to his car, a beat-up 1985 Honda Civic, which he bought for only $2,000. He wanted to get a new car when he started his new job, but that wasn't going to happen now.

Isaiah drove. He didn't know where he was going; he just drove and thought about school. School was not his thing. He didn't get into any more trouble than the next guy. Just the basic cutting-up-in-class kind of trouble. He had a few friends, and that is where he met Natasha. He just never studied. He wasn't stupid. He remembers one time *studying* for a history test, and he got a B+. He knew he could do the work if he wanted to. He simply didn't want to. Making money sounded better than being in class all day.

When he was 17, he was sent to alternative school so he could catch up. He was in a school where the "bad" kids were sent, but he was there so he could catch up on his work. He was 17 years old and still in the 9th grade. He dropped out of school because he felt embarrassed to be in the same classroom as 14- and 15-year-old punks who couldn't sit still for five minutes without cursing out the teacher. It was a waste of his time. He quit and got a job at a grocery store. He liked making his own money. And he didn't see the point in going back to school.

He had thought about getting his GED. Not for his benefit, but for his mother's. She wanted him to graduate, but a GED would be just as good. But by the time he got around to it, Natasha was pregnant, and he was hired at the DDC. The full-time job and trying to be a good dad left no time for studying for a stupid piece of paper.

Possible Approaches

Having a young man like Isaiah in your program would be great, but getting him into the program could be difficult. The initial contact you make with him will be crucial.

The most important thing you can do is help him see the big picture. He thinks getting a GED is a waste of time and money. But as a program coordinator or educator, you know the benefits of having a diploma or GED in today's job market. Help Isaiah establish his goals and objectives for the next year or two. Ask him what he would like to accomplish and where he sees himself in a year. Encourage him to put this down in writing including a time frame for meeting his goals.

If he can visualize the amount of time it will take to get his GED, as well as find another job, he may be more inclined to go along with your ideas and accept your help. Also, help him realize that getting his GED or even higher education will not only benefit him, but also Jessica.

His self-esteem also needs building. Losing an important job, one that he enjoyed and where he performed well, can take its toll on his feelings of self-worth. Tell him that he has proved he can do the work and handle the responsibility that a demanding job requires. Not too many fathers his age have done that.

Young men like Isaiah are self-sufficient, a good quality for a father to have. Isaiah would be an asset for the program because he would be a good role model for the other dads. Even though Isaiah lied on his application, he can model the work ethic. He can also help others understand the importance of telling the truth on an application.

Many young fathers face many obstacles in finding a good job. Isaiah has had a good job, and he can share his experiences with the group. However, he may not feel he needs your help or the group's support, so share with him how you and the group can help him, especially by encouraging him to continue his education.

Encourage Isaiah to join the support group and ask as often as you can for his input to be shared with the group. He will feel a sense of ownership and belonging that will keep him coming back. Brag about him and his accomplishments. I know of no one who does not like to be recognized for his work and efforts.

Help with GED, Job Search

Next is to get Isaiah thinking about his GED. Talk to him about his school experiences, his likes and dislikes. Help him understand the benefits of education. Take him to education centers that offer GED programs. Have counselors and educators talk to him about the requirements, class schedules, and procedures he will need to acquire his GED.

If he is afraid he cannot do the work, get him some tutoring. You may in fact be able to tutor him yourself in most subjects. There may be some programs that offer tutoring or the GED program may have tutoring available.

You might help Isaiah look into some apprenticeship programs or vocational schools. However, he might prefer to get into a program that enables him to learn while he works and receive a paycheck. Some programs provide education and on-the-job training as well as job placement. A drawback is these programs often pay minimum wage and pay only for the amount of time the employee works, perhaps only ten to twenty hours per week.

Do all you can to help him get a job. He may not appear to need your help in this area, but look out for him anyhow. He may have gone back to the grocery store or be working at a fast-food restaurant. If he is, that's fine. Isaiah, however, is used to making over $8 per hour, and making less money will affect his self-esteem. Help him find a job that enables him to spend time with his daughter, and one that will not hurt his ability to get a GED. He will appreciate that and feel that participating in your program is worthwhile.

The Child Support Issue

One final thing is extremely important. Most young fathers know nothing about the child support issue. Most courts make a father pay child support based on their income. If he was once making $8.25 per hour, and is now making $6.75 per hour, the money he has to live on will be decreased tremendously. Take Isaiah to court or to child support enforcement (normally it is child support enforcement) and ask for a reduction in payments. This is a normal procedure that many fathers don't realize they can follow.

Many fathers do not pay the amount that was set when they were working a higher paying job. This puts them in a terrible situation, because whatever they don't pay on schedule will have to be repaid at some later time. This can be devastating for any father. If Isaiah explains his reduced income to the case manager who handles his child support payments, they can reduce the amount he owes and he won't get behind in the payments. He'll still be providing for his daughter.

Accompany him to these meetings with the child support officials. Many times they are intimidating toward young fathers. Many young men come into our program and talk about how negatively they are treated when it comes to paying child support. Your presence at the meetings will prove that you are there for him. This simple gesture, which may take only an hour out of your busy schedule, will be beneficial for Isaiah.

3

Andre — No Desire to Parent . . . Then a Sudden Change

Andre placed the phone back on the receiver and walked into the kitchen to fix a sandwich. He was unfazed by the information he'd received.

"Andre, was that your sister calling?" his mother asked.

"No, Mom."

"Who was it?"

"That was Theresa's mom," he said.

"Well, is it time?"

"I guess," Andre said. "Actually it's past time. She had the baby this morning. A little boy."

Andre's mother looked him over. She couldn't tell if he was nervous, happy, angry; she couldn't see any emotion. "Are you going to the hospital?"

"I doubt it. She doesn't need me there," Andre said.

"Well, it's your responsibility now. You know you've got to provide for that new son of yours."

Andre finished his sandwich and put his plate in the sink. He thought about doing the dishes that were in the sink, looked at his watch, and decided he didn't have time. He was meeting his best friend at the high school football game. Andre graduated from school last summer, but he and "his boy" enjoyed going to the game to check out the girls.

Andre arrived at the bus stop in time to catch the metro going toward the high school. The neon sign let the passengers know their destination by showing "William Fleming High School." Andre paid the $1.25 fare, and found a seat in the back of the bus. He looked out the window and thought about the phone conversation.

"I'm a dad," he thought. It still didn't change the way he felt about the situation. He felt nothing. He was not interested in Theresa and was not interested in being a father. Andre had spent his whole life without a dad. He asked his mother about him once, and she told him his father was in prison. He asked no more questions. "He'll be okay," he thought. After all, he grew up without a father.

He had no desire to be with Theresa. He met her at a party one night, when she approached him. They talked and danced, and she was nice, he thought. A couple of days later, he went to her place and they had sex. It sounds so emotionless, but that is what it was, just sex. After they finished, he left.

He would go days without calling, and she wouldn't call him either. Whenever he wanted to be with a woman, he would place the "booty call." She had no problem with their arrangement, and this was his dream come true. Sex with no strings attached.

This relationship endured two months. One Saturday night, Andre picked up the phone to make his weekly call.

"What's up, girl?" Andre said in his most suave voice. "Is it alright if I come over?"

"I'm pregnant, Andre," Theresa told him. She came right out and told him; no emotion. She wasn't upset or happy. As a matter of fact, she already had two kids by two different fathers.

Andre stopped visiting. No more booty calls, no stopping by to see how she was doing or if she needed anything. He felt if he stopped calling, she would forget about their sexual encounters.

As the bus pulled into the stadium parking lot, Andre saw Kevin, his best friend, waiting by the entrance gate.

"Hey man, what's new?" Kevin asked.

"Nothing, man," Andre replied. "Nothing."

One Year Later

One year passed but little changed. Andre had been taken to court for child support. At the time of his court date, he had a pretty good job working for a laundry service. He was ordered to pay $125 per month. One week later, he quit because he didn't like his supervisor. Andre felt he singled him out for the jobs everyone else hated to do.

He had seen his son only two times. Once at the mall, and the other time when he had to appear in court. "He looks just like me," Andre thought. He still had no desire to spend time with his son. Andre thought his child was being taken care of because Andre was making child support payments, at least when he was working.

One evening Andre walked into his apartment after work. He had just gotten a job at a temporary employment agency working in a hospital cafeteria. It wasn't much, but it put money in his pocket every week, instead of every two weeks, like he'd been paid at the laundry service. He strolled into the kitchen to find something to eat. As he was preparing a snack of leftover meatloaf, he glanced at the table and noticed a letter with his name on it.

Dear Andre,

I know this may come as a shock to you after all these years. I have been writing this letter it seems for five years. Every time I start to write to you, the words never seem to come out right, so I start over. I don't know where to begin, so let's start from the beginning.

I want to apologize for not being in your life. I'm sorry. I wish there were some way I could make it up to you. But I know that will never happen. When your mother told me she was pregnant, I was young and into things a real man shouldn't be into. I was excited at the thought of being a father. I loved your mother very much, but that didn't change the way I lived my life. I would get drunk or high every night. Some nights, I would forget to come home.

One night, some things went down and a fight started, and I killed a man. It was an accident. I was so drunk I don't remember it to this day. Spending most of my life in prison hasn't been that bad. It's an adjustment, and I guess I've adjusted. The hardest thing is not being in yours and your mother's life. For that, I don't think I will ever adjust.

Son, if there is anything I can do to make this up to you, please let me know what it is. I want to be a part of your life, although from a distance. I think of you every day, and how your life could have been better if your mother had some help in raising you. I know she did fine without me, but I believe we could have done better together. If you could find it in your heart to come and visit or send me a letter letting me know how you are, I would be thankful.

                                                                Love, Your dad

Andre folded the letter and put it back in the envelope. He felt a tear falling down his cheek and quickly brushed it away. He picked up his jacket and walked toward the door.

"Where you going, baby?" his mother asked.

"I'll be right back, Mom."

Andre caught the metro across town to the apartment complex. As he walked up toward apartment 5E, he began to feel his heart beat. He gave the door a hard knock.

"What are you doing here?" Theresa asked.

"I'm here to see my son."

Possible Approaches

Having a father like Andre in your program can be a challenge and a test of will and patience. When Andre received the letter, it sparked something in him that made him want to visit his son. That is the result you want; however, the journey will not end there.

Andre had not been interested in having a relationship with his son. He paid his child support payments when he could, and he felt that he was doing enough. Many times, the system leads a young father to believe that if he pays child support, then he is doing his job. A child needs money to survive, but a father's love and involvement are irreplaceable.

Help with Parenting

Help Andre learn about one-year-olds so he can be comfortable when/if he spends time with his son. What does he know about disciplining (teaching) toddlers? Does he understand that gentle discipline rather than yelling or spanking will produce better results? Does he know the importance of reading to and talking with his son? You could also offer some quick information on nutrition for toddlers. If you don't offer parenting help directly, help him find a way to learn elsewhere.

Andre needs to participate in a support group. He needs to see other fathers involved in their children's lives. The support group is also a forum to allow Andre to put his feelings on the table and let the group help him deal with his anxieties. This will not happen at the first meeting. With consistent attendance, Andre will feel comfortable in the group and may disclose his story. As the educator, it is important that you allow time in each session to let the guys voice their concerns and problems.

Importance of Job Skills

Job skills are important to Andre's success as a man and a father. He has bounced around from one job to the next, quitting a decent job because of an overbearing supervisor. If a young man is taught the importance of steady work, he will take his jobs more seriously. If a young man can keep a job, even when things are stacked against him, it will foster more responsibility in other aspects of his life.

This doesn't mean you should recommend a guy stay with a job in which he is miserable or is being treated unfairly. But if he quits whenever something happens that he doesn't like, he's running away and not facing the adversities within the job. The same holds true for fatherhood. If your child does something that you don't like, you cannot walk away or quit. Help Andre enroll in a job training program. These programs offer aptitude tests, mock interviews, etc.

It's important that Andre make his child support payments. A young father who falls behind in payments will have a difficult time catching up later.

Make sure Andre understands the importance of avoiding STIs (sexually transmitted infections) and another unplanned pregnancy. In fact, this is a topic you need to cover frequently in your sessions with young fathers. Don't lecture as in "Don't ever have sex again until you're married." You will have more positive results if you initiate discussions in which the young men remind each other of the importance of using a condom *every time* they have sexual intercourse. Perhaps they could roleplay negotiating the use of a condom with a partner who doesn't think it's important.

There is no magic formula to get a father like Andre involved in his child's life. It may take a long time and a lot of patience. Encourage him to visit his son; tell him you will go with him. If he refuses, don't push. As long as he is in the group, he will know that he is not doing what a father is supposed to do.

At a friend's suggestion, Andre called us the day after his first visit with his son. With our encouragement, he started visiting his son regularly. Eventually, the visits turned into overnight sleepovers at his house. He would pick him up from daycare. He started working on a steady basis and caught up on his back child support payments. He bought clothes and shoes for his son. He even had a decent "communicating" relationship with the mother.

How did this happen? For Andre, something was triggered inside him, prompting him to go see his son. The interaction that he received from the other fathers in the support group and the trust that was built in those group sessions may have given him the strength to become more involved. The group always supported him, especially when he would brag about his new relationship with his son. He became a model father in our program.

The key is patience. We can't give up on a father like Andre. If we abandon him, he may never become an involved father. We may feel frustrated when guys like Andre are not making progress. If we support and guide him through his journey of becoming a dad, positive changes are likely to happen.

4

Greg — No Visitations
But Must Pay Child Support

Greg stood before the judge and was most uncomfortable. He had debated about not coming to court at all, but his mother convinced him otherwise. His ex-girlfriend had petitioned the court for child support. Greg had been in trouble with the law before. Nothing too serious — trespassing and driving without an operator's license. Nevertheless, he felt he had been abused both times, and he felt especially nervous now.

"Mr. Myers, do you have a job?" the judge asked.

"Yes, sir. Part-time," Greg responded.

The judge calculated how much Greg made, and how much the state guidelines required him to pay. He also listened to Heather explain how Greg never provided for their daughter. The exchange between the judge and Heather lasted for five minutes, but it felt like an hour to Greg. They were crucifying him in the courtroom, and the judge kept giving Greg dirty looks. He knew he had no chance.

"Mr. Myers, I'm ordering you to pay $25 per week. You can choose to pay every two weeks, or every month depending upon your pay schedule. You better make sure that Ms. Jenkins receives $100 per month, because if you don't, I'll lock you up for contempt of court. Do you understand me?"

"But sir, she won't let me see my daughter," Greg said, hoping to gain sympathy.

"Do you understand what I said?" the judge yelled.

Greg gave the judge a long, hard stare. He could feel the heat in his body as his muscles tensed.

"Yeah, I understand. But can I see my daughter?"

"That is for you two to work out. If you feel that you don't get enough time with your daughter, petition the court for another hearing. That is all," the judge said as he banged his gavel.

Greg walked out of the courtroom feeling more alone than he had ever felt before. The anger was still with him as he walked to the parking garage where his car was waiting. "That idiot judge wouldn't even listen to me," he thought. He had had it with the court system. Every time he has been to court, he has gotten nothing but disrespect.

Two Weeks Later

Greg walked out of the bank after cashing his paycheck of $93.76. This was the amount left after taxes. Taxes always ate his check, and he didn't know what most of the things were that were "stealing his money."

"What is FICA?" he thought to himself.

He got in his car and set aside $50 for child support and the rest went into his pocket. He grimaced at the thought of giving more than half of his paycheck to Heather. He exited the parking lot and proceeded to Heather's house.

Greg pulled in front of the house and started walking toward the door. He realized that he had forgotten the envelope and went back to his car to retrieve the money. He really hated to give her the money. Greg gave a quick knock. Her father answered the door and came out to the porch.

He gave Greg an evil look and yelled, "Heather, Greg's outside," without taking his eyes off Greg. He heard Heather coming down the steps.

"You got the money?" Heather asked.

WHAT? No "Hello, how are you?" All she asked was, "You got the money?"

"Yeah, I've got our daughter's money," Greg replied. He wondered how much would go toward his daughter. "Can I see her?"

"Now's not a good time, Greg. She's taking a nap."

"Every time I want to see her, she's taking a nap. If you don't let me see her, you're not getting the money."

"Why are you always so difficult?" Heather asked.

"I just want to see my daughter. She's my daughter, too," Greg said as calmly as he could.

Heather went inside and brought their daughter, Sarah, out with her. She always brought Sarah outside instead of letting Greg come inside. Sarah was eight months old. She had big green eyes and her brown hair was starting to fill out. She resembled Greg, and he liked the fact that his daughter looked like him.

He rarely was "allowed" to see his daughter. Since she had been born, Greg may have seen her five times. Heather's dad thought it would be best for everyone if Greg didn't spend time with Sarah. He didn't like Greg, but Greg understood. "I'd be mad if somebody knocked up my daughter, too," he had said.

"When can I take her home to spend the night?" Greg asked.

"Spend the night? Are you crazy? You don't know the first thing about taking care of a child. I'm not letting my baby stay in your house."

"My mom will be there, she knows how to handle babies," Greg said. "And I think you mean 'our' child."

"Never!" Heather said.

"Then we'll go to court. I have a right to see my daughter."

Heather was about to speak when her father took Sarah out of his arms and said, "Greg, what judge is going to give you visitation rights? You are sixteen years old, have been arrested, and can barely keep a job. No judge, especially the one we had last time, would give you anything."

Greg knew he was beat. He was so mad, he thought about throwing a punch at Heather's dad, but he was holding Sarah. Greg turned to walk away when Heather yelled at him.

"Hey, Greg, aren't you forgetting something?"

"Oh yeah, the money," Greg replied, less than enthusiastically. Oh yeah, the money.

Possible Approaches

Greg did not want to pay the child support. Who can blame him? In the article, "Examining the Connection between Child Access and Child Support" *(Family and Conciliation Courts Review*, January 1994, v. 32, p. 93), Jessica Pearson and Jean Anhalt concluded from a survey that, "One quarter of non-custodial fathers agree with the statement, 'If I were visiting my children more regularly, I would feel more like paying child support.'" Greg wanted badly to spend time with his child, but was thwarted by Heather's father. This is a common problem for teen fathers. It can be difficult to deal with his baby's mother, but overwhelming when he has to deal with the whole family.

When you contact a young father like Greg, he may be very willing to join your young fathers program. He has no options, and has a great disdain for the court system. He feels that he will lose if he goes back to court. When you fill out a needs assessment survey on Greg, legal help will be a big topic of conversation. It is very important to let him know that you will do everything in your power to provide legal assistance.

Don't promise him things you can't provide, such as a lawyer. If your program has an attorney, that's great. If you tell him you will get him something, however, and don't come through, he will lose faith in you and the program, and may stop participating.

Airing Frustrations

The first step in helping Greg is, of course, the support group. The support group is a great place for Greg to air out his feelings and frustrations. Other fathers may be in the same predicament as Greg. Their understanding will make it easier for Greg to deal with his separation from his daughter, as well as the mistreatment from the judicial system.

The support groups are a great place for a lawyer to come in and give the group an educational session on their rights as fathers. You can prepare your fathers by having them write questions to ask your guest speaker. Your guest should be supportive of father's rights. It would be disastrous to have

someone speak to your group and give a lecture on
"deadbeat dads."

Filing a Court Petition

The next thing you can do is accompany Greg to the
courthouse and help him fill out the proper documents in order to
petition the court for a visitation hearing. This can be a pretty
intimidating experience for a father of any age. Before you take
him, go by yourself or with other educators and counselors
within your program, to familiarize yourself with the process.

If you don't know how to file a petition, be prepared to go
from one office to another until you find what you're looking
for. We spent hours in the Roanoke courthouse trying to
determine what needs to be done so the fathers from our group
can take the necessary steps to gaining parental rights. Try to
keep your cool in this situation. As you are directed from one
office to the next, you may understand why many fathers don't
want to go to court.

Next, accompany Greg to court on the date of his hearing.
You may be able to speak for him (though not always). The
ROAD program has a good reputation with some of the Juvenile
and Domestic Relations Court judges, and counselors are at
times allowed to speak on behalf of a young father. Even if you
are not allowed to speak for your client, your support will speak
volumes for Greg.

Before the above approaches are taken, find a lawyer who can
advise you and the fathers on issues pertaining to child support,
visitation, and custody. Some lawyers will provide services pro-
bono. However, lawyers are extremely busy, and many times are
being courted by other people requesting help at no charge.

There may also be a legal service, such as Legal Aid, that
provides representation to clients based on their income. The
downside, once again, is they are often bombarded with
other requests.

You can do the research yourself. Familiarize yourself with
state laws concerning visitation and child support. You can also
buy books on the subject. *Fathers' Rights* by Jeffery M. Leving
et al. (1998: Basic Books) gives great insight to what fathers

should do when involved in a custody conflict. *Child Custody Made Simple* by Webster Watnik (1999: Single Parent Press) also offers good practical advice on what fathers can do to become more involved with their children when the courts are involved.

Parenting a Toddler

Encourage Greg to learn about parenting babies and toddlers. Visits with his daughter will go better if he knows something about her development and needs. Does he realize that her first and most used word may be "No," and some of the ways parents can handle this stage without getting upset with their child? Does he already know how to play with a child this age, the activities she's most likely to enjoy?

Perhaps next time he takes the support money to Heather, he could call first and ask when his daughter will be awake. He might offer to bring a picture book with him, and tell Heather he'd like to show it to Sarah. If Heather and her parents see Greg playing a positive role with his daughter, they will be more likely to accept him as her father.

5

Jacob — Court Orders Counseling Before He Sees His Daughter

Julie's pager has been going off all morning long. The first page came through at 7 a.m., then at 7:30, 7:45, and 8:00. All of the pages ended in 911. Julie had her pager in her car, and didn't see the pages until she had loaded her children in the car and was on her way to drop them off at school.

After she saw her children through the school door, she was able to return the call at 8:23 a.m. Jacob answered the phone, slightly out of breath. "Julie?" He didn't even say hello. "I've been paging you all morning."

Julie, a caseworker for the ROAD program, hadn't even had her first cup of coffee and it was Monday. Not a good way to start the week. "Hey, Jacob," she said in as cheerful a voice as she could muster. "I just dropped my kids off at school. Is everything okay?"

"NO! I went for my supervised visitation this week and they wouldn't let me see Dorothy. They say I'm too angry and I need counseling before I can see her again. How am I going to pay for counseling? And who are THEY to tell me I can't see my daughter. The judge said . . . "

"Jacob, please calm down. I'll be over in a minute and we can talk then, okay?"

After a moment of silence, Jacob conceded. "Okay, but I've got to be at work by 10."

Julie stopped by the coffee shop on her way to Jacob's place. This is not the first frantic call she has received from him. The first time he called, he was in jail. He had been locked up because he had broken the restraining order against his ex-girlfriend, Patty. "All I wanted to do was talk to her," Jacob explained.

The second call was about the child support order he received in the mail. The judge had ordered Jacob to pay $200 per month on a minimum wage job. "I can't afford to live if I pay $200 per month," he pleaded. There were several other calls, and this one was no different. Julie tried to think of how to calm him down and explain what needed to be done.

Jacob had been involved with Patty for about two years. After Dorothy was born, their relationship deteriorated, and he felt helpless. He desperately wanted it to work, but his drinking and temper didn't help matters. He had loved Patty like no other, and she destroyed his heart. He wanted a family more than anything, but Patty had other plans. While he was at work, she was seeing a new guy. Unbeknown to Jacob, she had plans to leave him. He thought everything was fine until one day she asked him to leave.

"Where is this coming from?" he asked her. "I love you. I want to marry you."

His last ditch effort was in vain, for she had her mind made up. It was over.

From the time Jacob joined the fathers program, his emotions often came out. He once stormed out of a support group because the facilitator tried to move to another participant. Jacob only wanted to talk about his problems, and the rest of the group was getting weary of hearing his complaining. He was controlling the group, and the facilitator tried to move on to incorporate the other fathers. Jacob saw the facilitator's actions as disrespectful, and vowed never to return. It wasn't until Julie paid him a visit to explain why the other fathers needed to participate that he agreed to give it another shot.

Julie pulled in front of Jacob's apartment building. As she was walking up the stairs she heard Jacob's door open. He must have been watching for her car. When she walked in, he was sitting on the couch smoking a cigarette. Julie hated cigarettes, but she reminded herself she was in his home, so she said nothing. "So what happened, Jacob?"

Jacob explained how he showed up for his visitation on Saturday morning. Joyce, the visitation program supervisor, pulled him into her office and told him that he couldn't see Dorothy this weekend because of his recent behavior. Joyce reminded him of the restraining order. She also noticed that on the last visit, he cried almost the entire visit with his daughter, and that this had upset the little girl. Joyce told him he would have to see a counselor before the visits could be resumed.

"Just because I'm an emotional guy, they say I can't see my daughter. They have no right to keep me from my daughter."

Julie excused herself and called Joyce to learn her side of the story. Joyce informed her of phone contacts and letters that Jacob had sent to Patty, and of remarks that Jacob made concerning Patty's new relationship. Joyce explained that Jacob had been extremely emotional and might need to work some things out with a counselor. Julie told Joyce that she would make some calls and get back to her.

Julie went back into the living room where Jacob had started another cigarette. "Jacob, we need to talk," she said.

"I don't want to go to counseling," said Jacob. "I've been to counseling before and it didn't do any good."

"Jacob, listen to me. I think it's a good idea for you to see a counselor."

"Oh, not you, too."

"No, no. Hear me out. Ever since you joined the program, you've talked about your relationship with your daughter and about your experience as a father, and you've never gotten emotional. But when we talk about Patty, you always seem to get upset. I think if you could talk to a counselor, it would help you sort out the feelings you have about Patty, because if you don't, it could get the best of you later on."

"But why won't she talk to me? I only want an explanation for what happened. Don't I deserve that?"

"No." Julie said it very bluntly, almost hatefully. "Jacob, you guys have been apart for over six months. I agree with you that she did you wrong, but the thing is, she doesn't owe you anything except an opportunity to be a father to Dorothy. Jacob, I have no doubt that you love your daughter more than anything, but I also know that you have a lot of anger built up inside of you, and if you don't talk to a professional, it's going to get worse."

Jacob sat in silence, staring at the floor.

"I want to help you, but you have to *let* me help you. You've been in the program for three months, and you haven't taken any of my advice. Have I always been straight with you?"

"Yes."

"Have I always been honest with you?"

"Yes, you have."

"Then take my advice and see a counselor. The program has an agency that we refer dads to all the time. What do you say? Will you trust us to help you?"

"Yeah, I'll try."

Possible Approaches

Jacob is going through an extremely difficult time and needs as much support as possible. The way you or your staff handle his situation will be critical to him in getting through his emotional state.

Jacob has been in the program for several months now and has made little progress dealing with the court system, child support, his visitation center, and especially his child's mother. Julie has worked extensively with Patty with some success, but the ROAD staff is not making a lot of headway. Jacob simply can't see the light at the end of the tunnel. Nothing seems to be going his way, and he is at a point of desperation. If he fails to see results soon, he will be more likely to leave the program. The same holds true for any father. If they are not receiving services or if they do not see anything working for them, they will see no point in continuing.

Earning Jacob's trust is critical to his success. Keep working with him. You may find you need to be passive and listen . . . or if that doesn't work, perhaps a more aggressive approach will be more satisfactory for Jacob. The way you interact with a father like Jacob depends on his personality and the time you can put into the relationship.

Need Counselors on Call

The first step is to set him up with counseling. It is imperative that you have a list of counselors that you can contact in these situations. Find counselors that specialize in various areas such as substance abuse, domestic violence, conflict resolution, mediation, and general counseling services.

Some counseling services will assist your clients at a reduced rate. Always ask if this is an option. If they cannot give you the counseling at a reduced rate, ask if they can give your clients preference when they see them. (Counselors are often very busy, and it could take weeks before your client is seen.)

Make sure you establish a relationship with a counselor before you need it. Supply plenty of information about your program, and you may want to draft a memorandum of understanding (MOU). The MOU could state that their agency will give your participants a preferred rate or some preferential treatment. You will, however, need to sign release of information forms for each client, and have each client sign his form as well. Make a copy of this form for the participant's file. This will be good collaboration, and your program will be stronger as a result of the partnership.

Once you set up the counseling for Jacob, ask if you or someone from your program can accompany him to an initial meeting to introduce him to the counselor. This may help Jacob feel comfortable with the counselor, and this show of support will show him that you have his best interest at heart.

The second thing is to set up the appointment with Joyce, the visitation supervisor. When you schedule the meeting, take Jacob's file so you can accurately articulate the extent of his involvement. You must also have a date established for the counseling session. Give her the information concerning the counselor that will be seeing Jacob.

You may have to sign some documents stating the agencies can talk about Jacob and his progress. You will need Jacob's consent, and that shouldn't be a problem. This will protect everyone involved when it comes to confidentiality.

While you're meeting with Joyce, get an exact date that Jacob can resume his visitation with his daughter. Be adamant about that. You must be a strong advocate for Jacob. Remember that he must see a light at the end of the tunnel.

Finding Legal Help

The third thing to do, if at all possible, is find a lawyer that will represent him in his restraining order case. Hopefully you can find a lawyer who will represent your clients pro-bono. Jimmy Robinson, an attorney with Gentry, Locke, Rakes, and Moore, represents ROAD participants who are in good standing or past graduates. To be in good standing they have to be working toward their stated goals and faithfully attending the support group meetings. Jimmy represents our fathers only on cases concerning matters related to their children such as visitation, support orders, or custody cases. The restraining order may be a bit of a stretch, but it is directly related to Jacob's family.

If you don't have a lawyer on call, contact Legal Aid and ask if they will take the case. You can accompany Jacob to court and talk about the good things he has done in the program. Having legal representation for your participants is an invaluable asset to any program. If it weren't for Jimmy, many of our fathers would have been denied visitation or other simple rights that are often denied to fathers, particularly very young dads.

Peer Mentor Can Help

The last thing to do is introduce Jacob to other participants or graduates who have succeeded, despite insurmountable odds. Let that participant mentor Jacob and offer helpful advice. A peer mentor may be more effective than you or anyone on your staff. D.C. Dunnaville was one of the first graduates of our program. He was anything but a model father when he joined ROAD. He would not even participate in support group conversations. D.C., whose story is told on pages 26-27, has been extremely important in mentoring the young men in ROAD. He can give the guys a clearer picture of what to expect. He's "been there, done that," and the young fathers respect that.

The most important factor is time. Move as quickly as possible. Time is of the essence. Julie had to get a little forceful with Jacob, and you will have to determine if that is the best approach for your client. You can't take the direct approach with every dad, but some need and even want that type of intervention.

He needs help in developing job skills and the desire to work.

6

Juan — Jobless Again. "They Don't Treat Me Right So I Quit"

Juan held the business card in his hands. He didn't want to use it, but Jennifer said if he wanted to be with her, he'd have to make the call. Juan had held out as long as he could, using every possible excuse just so she wouldn't leave him.

Jennifer was the perfect girl. She had stayed with him through the good times and the bad, although there were a lot more bad than good. She was there when he dropped out of school, but she encouraged him to get his GED. She was there the time he was arrested for selling crack. She even bailed him out of jail. She was there when he got fired from Krispy Kreme Donuts, even though it was only his third day on the job. He even cheated on her a couple of times, but she always took him back.

Juan sat there thinking about making the call, and wondering why she had stayed with him for so long. *Megan* was the reason she had stayed and kept on trying to save their relationship even though he wasn't putting forth the effort. Megan was their daughter, a beautiful ten-month-old baby with dark eyes and black hair. This time though, he had really messed up. Jennifer threatened him that if he didn't make the call, they were through.

Last week Juan got a job at a local bowling alley. It was easy work. He was the guy who took the money and gave the customers those ugly clown-looking bowling shoes, but he was fired after only two days. He didn't come into work the third evening because there was a bunch of guys playing ball at the gym. Juan knew he needed to be at work, but he was having so much fun playing basketball, he decided to ditch work. He didn't think he would get fired for it. So now he sat next to the phone and looked at the business card. Finally, he picked up the phone and dialed the number.

A man answered the phone on the first ring. "ROAD Father's Program," the man said, his voice upbeat and energetic. "This is Barry, can I help you?"

Juan sat for a moment, then replied, "Yeah, my girlfriend gave me your card and said I should give you a call."

"Are you a father?" Barry asked.

"Yes, I have a daughter."

Barry and Juan talked for about fifteen minutes. Juan told Barry about Megan and his relationship with Jennifer. Juan also told Barry that he needed a job and was kind of desperate.

"Nobody will hire me," said Juan. "The jobs I've had, I haven't liked because they don't treat me right, so I quit." Barry documented the information and set up a meeting with Juan for the next day.

Barry came to the house to talk with Juan about some job possibilities. The idea of getting a job without having to beg excited Juan. That was the most humiliating part of looking for work. He hated it when they told him, "Sorry, but we're not hiring." But before Juan became too excited, Barry burst his bubble.

"These contacts are a place for you to start, but they are not just going to give you a job. You have to apply and interview like everyone else. They will give you preferential consideration if my name is on the application, but you need to understand that if you use my name, I expect you to do your best. I will give you a ride and help you out as much as I can. Does that sound okay?"

"Yeah, that sounds good," Juan said. He still had to work for it, which he didn't like too well, but it was all he had.

The next day, Barry picked Juan up at Jennifer's house, and they went to fill out applications. Juan did just as Barry advised and put his name under the "references" section of the application. They rode all over town filling out applications. Juan figured he would be working by the end of the week.

Nothing happened. No phone calls from any of the places they had visited. Jennifer was starting to get on his case again about not working. He waited for two weeks and nothing happened. Barry had even dropped off some more applications for him to fill out. Nothing came of those either. Jennifer was beginning to get impatient with Juan's continued unemployment.

"The baby needs diapers and clothes," she yelled. "How come I can work all day, come home, take care of the baby, and all you do is hang out with your friends?"

"It's not my fault," Juan screamed back. "It's Barry's fault. He said he would get me a job. I've filled out applications and no one has called me back. It's not my fault."

Jennifer stood in the middle of the room and stared at her feet. She was fed up and Juan could tell. "If you don't start helping me out with some money, we're through. I'm doing it by myself now, so if you can't help, then don't bother coming home."

Juan walked out of the house feeling dejected. He had failed again, and if he didn't come through, Jennifer would leave him. He could tell she was serious this time. She'd had enough. He walked so he could clear things up in his mind. "How am I going to get some money for Jennifer and the baby?" he thought. He walked and walked, trying to think of what he could do.

When Jennifer awoke the next day, Juan was not there. "He probably stayed the night with a friend," she thought. He had often done that without letting her know. As she was getting ready for work, the phone rang. "That better be him," she said.

"Jennifer," Juan said. "Uh, I messed up again."

"What are you talking about? Did you cheat on me again?"

"No, I didn't," Juan said. She could tell by the sound of his voice something was wrong. "I'm in jail."

"Oh, Juan." Jennifer began to cry. "Drugs?"

"Yeah, drugs."

Possible Approaches

Young men like Juan find it very difficult to keep a job. This is because they lack a sense of responsibility. Juan needs guidance, education, and most of all, patience from you. Young men like Juan will not be quick to change simply because they enroll in your program. As a matter of fact, the ROAD program has dealt with several fathers who cannot keep a job. As educators or caseworkers, however, we can't give up on young men like Juan.

First of all, Juan wanted to get a job so Jennifer wouldn't leave him. He seemed more interested in keeping her than providing for his daughter.

Getting Juan involved in the support group is important because it will help him to see other young men his age being involved in their child's life. We need to direct Juan's focus away from Jennifer and toward his child. This doesn't mean he should break up with her or abandon her, because he seems to be in love with her. However, many parents make the mistake of putting their love or social life before the needs of their children. If we can get Juan to realize this, he may be more focused on keeping his job.

Another approach to investigate is the child support issue. Currently, Juan does not have a child support order against him. This actually makes it easier for him to get away with not giving Jennifer money, as he should.

Remember that Jennifer has taken him back time after time. He may not believe that she would actually leave him if he doesn't work. However, if a judge orders him to pay child support every month, he may be more inclined to keep a job once he obtains one.

The ROAD program has helped teenage mothers file petitions seeking child support from fathers like Juan. Usually this encourages the fathers to keep jobs and pay their monthly amount on a regular basis. This approach can be dangerous, however, because it can cause the young father to resent you and leave your program. However, the welfare of the child must be the first priority.

Help with Job Applications, Interviews

Juan also needs education and help in obtaining a job. Barry picked him up and drove him to various businesses to look for employment, a good service to provide the fathers.

Sometimes a young man needs guidance on dressing for job-hunting. We have taken young dads out to look for work, and they were dressed in baseball caps, oversized T-shirts, and baggy jeans that hung off their backside. This wardrobe is perfectly okay for a young man who is hanging out with his friends, but it will not win over a manager reviewing his application.

The ROAD program now has a policy regarding the way a young man dresses when looking for work. If he doesn't have pants that come up to his waist, and a shirt that is tucked in, we will not take him job-hunting that day. He does not have to wear a tie, but he must shower, comb his hair, and dress in a presentable manner.

Other components of a good employment education program include teaching interviewing skills and providing advice on filling out an application properly. You can practice these skills in a support group setting or in the young man's home. Many young men do not complete the application properly or they write the information down so sloppily a manager can't read it.

You may need to sit down and watch him fill out the applications and help him in the areas where he needs help. Also, help him do some practice interviews. Teach him how to look in the interviewer's eye and talk in clear language that is loud enough to be heard. If an applicant does not speak in a clear tone, the manager may not think he is right for the job.

The Drug Issue

You and Juan need to deal with the issue of selling drugs. Young men often resort to this method of "employment" when jobs are hard to find. Some young men prefer that lifestyle as opposed to legal employment. Let Juan know you expect him not to deal drugs. It puts him in danger, but more importantly, Jennifer and the baby, too. Set the bar high for your participants. Be straight with Juan — don't sugarcoat the message. A drug dealer is not a good role model for children, particularly if he's in jail, or worse, dead!

A final thing you can do to help a young man like Juan is to visit him at his place of employment. Most employers will not mind an occasional visit, but remember to check with the manager. You do not want to be the reason that he loses his job. If a young man expects you to come by his job and check on him from time to time, he will be more inclined to be at work and do a good job, so he doesn't let you down. The ROAD program uses this practice, especially with younger fathers or young men who have a hard time keeping a job.

7

Jeremy — He and Tami
Are Getting Married

The fathers filtered into the meeting room one by one and
headed straight for the dinner table. Tonight was pasta night and
the young men loved the sauce La'Cove Restaurant donated.
La'Cove was one of the generous establishments that donated
often to the fathers program. Most nights, the young men would
greet each other and the counselors, but this was "Pasta Night."
Jeremy entered the room just as everyone else, heading straight
for the dinner table. Small talk among the young men was taking
place as the counselors were going around to each father and
welcoming them.

After the participants received more than a healthy portion,
they left the dinner table and came to the circle. The ROAD
Program incorporated the circle last fall. The staff felt the fathers
didn't open up to each other as easily when seated at the dinner
table. In the circle, the dads are closer to one another and feel
more comfortable talking about their situation.

Once the dads come to the circle, they open the meeting by
talking about anything significant that happened during the last
week. Joey talked about problems he was having on the job. Lee
talked about his disdain for his probation officer and the hard

time he was getting from him. Tyrone talked about how relieved he felt at being accepted in college. Jeremy, however, dropped a bomb on everyone.

"Well, I got engaged," he said.

The room was silent. The fathers didn't know what to say to him.

"Well congratulations, Jeremy," said Craig, one of the counselors for the ROAD Program. "That's great."

Craig started clapping and everyone else soon followed. Craig didn't exactly feel happy for Jeremy; he didn't know what to feel. As a matter of fact, Jeremy himself didn't exactly look thrilled at the thought of getting married.

After the group discussion, most of the guys hung around talking to Jeremy about his engagement. This was pretty deep for the participants to grasp. First of all, they knew of no one their age that was married. Jeremy was only 18 and Tami, his girlfriend, was 17. Second, they have heard Jeremy talk about the problems that he and Tami have experienced over the past three months. Third, Jeremy was working on his GED and was working hard for the city's Parks and Recreation Department. It was temporary employment mowing the parks around the city. Fourth, Jeremy is white and Tami is black. Jeremy has often talked about the way his family treats Tami and the way Tami's mom treats him. Actually, a lot of their fights have been based on their families' reaction toward Tami getting pregnant. Both Jeremy and Tami were not treated well by their future in-laws. Both families had problems with their child dating outside their race.

As the young men filtered out, Jeremy stayed behind. Craig was cleaning up the leftover bread and pasta when he saw Jeremy looking out the window. "Jeremy's gonna get married," Craig boasted. "You know you'll be the first in the program to get married. Are we invited?"

"Of course you're invited. All the guys are."

"So how did all this happen?" Craig asked. "I mean last week you were talking about how her mom didn't want you coming to the house to see her."

"Well, it happened kind of quick," Jeremy started. "My mom called Tami and said she would pay for an abortion. Tami paged me and she was crying. She didn't understand why my mom would call her and ask her to do that, especially this late. So she snuck out of her house and we met down at the park and started talking about how our families were keeping us apart. We started talking about how great it would be if we could live together so we wouldn't have to hear the put downs all the time. Then we started talking about marriage, so I asked her to marry me and she said 'yes.'"

Craig sat silent for a moment as if he was in deep thought. "So have you guys set a date for this?"

"We want to do it before the baby's born, and it's due in about five months. I want my baby to have my last name."

Jeremy helped Craig finish cleaning and straightening the chairs. Craig offered Jeremy a ride home. They small talked most of the way about sports and about Jeremy's job. Jeremy was hoping that they would keep him on the job after his temporary employment ended. They pulled in front of Jeremy's apartment building; Jeremy opened the car door and stepped out. He thanked Craig for the ride and shook his hand.

"Do you love her?" asked Craig.

"She's going to have my baby. I mean, yeah, I love her."

Possible Approaches

This situation may not come up often, but when it does, be prepared for it.

Craig did the right thing in the group. He turned an uncertain and awkward situation into a happy one by clapping and showing support for Jeremy. The other fathers didn't know how to react and neither did Craig. By clapping, he was showing Jeremy that he supported his decision, at least in front of the group.

If you are confronted with a young man telling you he is getting married and you don't approve, the support group is not the place to share your feelings. Actually, if you feel they should not get married, approach the discussion carefully. You don't want to sound like another parent or family member who has disapproved of their relationship from the start.

The first thing you do as a counselor is talk to Jeremy in a comfortable setting. Go to his home and talk to him alone, without interference from anyone else, including Tami. Ask him why he wants to get married. Ask him where he sees their relationship in five or ten years. Don't criticize; simply listen and try to get his real feelings on the situation.

Talk to him about the problems Tami and he are having. Will their problems stop when they are married or will they continue? How will being married help solve their problems? What do they need to work on before they get married?

Considering Financial Support

How will he support his family? This is extremely important to discuss because many young couples don't think about the financial impact they will face being on their own. A lot of teenagers take for granted all the bills that their parents pay while they are living under their parents' roof.

The ROAD program implements an activity titled, "Show Me the Money." The activity asks the participants to prepare a budget of their expected monthly expenses. The areas on which they will need to focus include:

• Rent or mortgage
• Childcare

- Food including formula (unless Tami breastfeeds completely)
- Diapers, baby clothes, and miscellaneous baby expenses
- Electricity, heating (natural gas or coal), and other utilities
- Phone bill (cellular as well)
- Cable
- Credit cards
- School loans
- Medical
- Entertainment (movies, CDs, theme parks)
- Clothing

After they write down their monthly projections, ask them what type of job they plan to have and how much they will get paid per hour. Ask them how much training or education they will need to make that much money. Once they figure out their chosen career and their hourly wage, compare their monthly income to the expenditures. Once the figures are compiled, take out 25 percent of their monthly income for taxes. If they do not plan to marry their child's mother, take out a couple of hundred dollars for child support or items for the child such as diapers, formula, toys, clothes, etc. This can be a sobering exercise for the young men.

This would be a good activity to do with Jeremy in his home or in the group setting. Plan a meeting with a money manager or credit counselor. Have Tami along for this activity. The credit counselor will help Jeremy and Tami establish a budget within their means.

Talk with an Interracial Couple?

The next thing you could do is introduce Jeremy and Tami to an interracial couple. Interracial couples are becoming more common, and in most places are perfectly acceptable. However, many families still hold prejudices about dating outside one's race.

If Jeremy and Tami can talk to a couple that has experienced the negativity, it may help them understand what they may face.

More importantly, this could help them figure out how they can deal with any pressures they encounter. If Jeremy and Tami don't want to talk to another couple, that's okay. Simply have the option available to them.

Jeremy needs to stay focused on his GED and furthering his education. Many young men quit school or drop out "temporarily" when they learn that they will be a father. This may be a quick fix but it is not the best thing for Jeremy or his family in the long-term.

Refer to Marriage Counselor

Suggest that Jeremy and Tami talk to a marriage counselor or minister, and offer to help them find one. Many churches and church-based organizations offer pre-marital counseling. This is a perfect opportunity for your organization to establish collaborations with the faith-based community.

It is important to establish relationships with several religious groups such as Baptist, Methodist, Catholic, Unitarian, Jewish, Muslim, and non-denominational churches. You must have several contacts because your participants will not all be of the same religion and some may not be religious at all. It is important to make them feel comfortable when talking to a minister or any person offering counseling. Having a relationship with many churches will only strengthen your organization, particularly when writing grants or building community support.

The last and most important thing you can do is support Jeremy and Tami's decision. You may not agree with their decision, but your support will be extremely important to them. They may experience negative feedback from family and friends, and they will not need the same pressure from you.

Let them know you will always be there for them. Help them obtain things that they may need for their home such as dishes, furniture, linens, etc. You may be able to obtain these articles by asking people in your office to donate unused or unwanted items. Your support of Jeremy and Tami will strengthen your bond with Jeremy and, most important, help them strengthen their relationship.

8

Anthony — Nowhere to Go

It was raining again. Whenever he got comfortable, it always seemed to start raining. If it wasn't raining, it was snowing. Foul weather would disturb him, wake him out of a dead sleep, or keep him from getting there. At times though, it wasn't that bad. He had gotten used to sleeping wherever he could lay his head, under the bridge, behind the Wal-Mart, and even on park benches. The best place he found to sleep was in the dugouts of the local baseball fields. Some of the dugouts even had a roof over the bench, which made for a good night's sleep.

As he woke with the rain falling on his face, he realized how hungry he was. He had missed dinner at the Rescue Mission because he found some of his friends to hang out with. That was the problem. His "friends."

Anthony used to have an okay life. Not perfect, and to some not good at all, but to others, it was definitely okay. Anthony lived with his mother until he was five years old. He adored his mother, but she was always strung out on some kind of drug. She did her best to keep it from him, but even at five years old, he knew. She died of a drug overdose in their apartment one week before Christmas. Everyone tried to keep from him the cause of his mother's death, but he knew. He still remembers that night, of being taken away by social services.

Anthony was somewhat lucky because he was placed immediately with a good foster family. Mr. and Mrs. Jenkins had a modest three bedroom home in the suburbs, and they had taken in many foster children over the years. The Jenkins were great to Anthony. They bought him clothes, toys, supported him when he played sports, and were actively involved in his education. They treated him as their own child, and people on the outside often didn't know that he was their foster child. Mrs. Jenkins never told people any different.

Anthony really liked Mrs. Jenkins but he wasn't that close to Mr. Jenkins. Mr. Jenkins was a good guy, but like many fathers in America, he was addicted to his work. Mr. Jenkins had three jobs, and the only time he really spent with Anthony was at the breakfast table before school and on Sundays. At first, Anthony was always trying to impress Mr. Jenkins, but after a while, he stopped.

Anthony's life started to go downhill when he was 14. He was hanging out with the wrong crowd, his "friends." Smoking weed and petty theft were taking up much of his spare time. He started having sex with anyone he could get with. He even caught syphilis one time, but that didn't change his behavior. He felt that since he "got that taken care of" with a shot, he could always do it again.

By this time, things had gone bad at home. He was caught stealing from his foster parents several times. He used the money from his parents' belongings to buy drugs. First weed, but then he progressed to heroin, ecstasy, and anything else he could get his hands on. He often bragged, "There ain't many drugs I ain't done."

Mr. and Mrs. Jenkins finally had enough of trying to raise him, so they gave him an ultimatum, "Get your life together or get out!" So Anthony left one night. No good-bye, nothing. He figured all they cared about anyway was the money social services was giving them.

At 17, Anthony was homeless and the father of two children

aged 18 months and 12 months. He stayed where he could when he could but his friends still lived at home with their parents, so they could only let him stay a couple of nights.

Anthony was walking on the street one day and came by the ROAD program office. He saw the sign on the door and decided to walk inside. Besides, he was a father so he thought he would check it out. Inside he met Jacob, one of the counselors for the program. Jacob approached him with his hand stretched out saying, "Hey there, I'm Jacob. How are you?"

Anthony shook his hand. "Do you help people find places to live?"

"We sure can," answered Jacob. "Are you a father?"

"Yeah, I have two kids."

Anthony entered the program and told Jacob of his situation. Jacob called the Rescue Mission to see if Anthony could stay there for a couple of days. The Rescue Mission informed Jacob that Anthony had been there before but he had been kicked out because he was fighting with another resident. Jacob called the other homeless shelters in town and found that Anthony had been kicked out of each one. Jacob's last call was to the Salvation Army. They didn't want Anthony either. Anthony hadn't stayed there but the Rescue Mission called and told them of the incident he had with another resident and advised them not to accept him. Jacob pleaded with them and told the Salvation Army that Anthony was now in the ROAD program, and he would help with case management. The Salvation Army reluctantly agreed.

Jacob told Anthony he had two weeks to get a job or the Salvation Army would kick him out. He also counseled him on his anger issues and informed him that an anger management class met at the office every week.

"The requirements for the program are you have to attend two job readiness classes and our fatherhood support group meetings," Jacob told him. "We expect you to keep in touch with us, and we will help you find a job. We want you to also pay child support and get more involved in your children's lives. Does that sound okay to you?"

"Yeah, I can do that."

Anthony attended the first job readiness class and the first support group meeting. He was extremely withdrawn except when the issue came to drug use. He defended people that used drugs saying, "It doesn't hurt anybody, and if God didn't want people to smoke weed, he wouldn't have put it on the earth."

Jacob saw Anthony every day for the first week he was enrolled. Anthony was working at Job Starts, a local company that employed people on a daily basis. The good thing about Job Starts is the employees get paid every day. This is beneficial to a guy like Anthony who needs money immediately. Jacob suggested that Anthony should be working with the employment specialist in the program to find full-time permanent employment. Job Starts does not guarantee work every day, and child support payments are not deducted from the employee's check. Also, it does not count as permanent employment.

The next week, however, was a different story. Anthony didn't show up for the job readiness class and he missed the support group. He had two meetings scheduled with Jacob and missed both of those as well. Jacob called the Salvation Army and they said Anthony had been leaving at the same time every morning and returning about the same time every night. As far as they knew, he was working.

The following week, Anthony walked into the office. "Man, where have you been?" Jacob asked. "I've been looking everywhere for you."

"I got kicked out of the shelter today," answered Anthony. "They tried to say I wasn't working."

Jacob called the Salvation Army and talked about Anthony's situation. Jacob was told that Anthony didn't work at all the previous week, and Job Starts didn't count as employment anyway. Jacob told them that he didn't come to any meetings the previous week so they hadn't been able to offer job services to him. Jacob asked for another chance for Anthony, but the Salvation Army said it was not fair to other residents who were trying to work.

Jacob talked to Anthony for a while and called the Homeless

Assistance Team. The HAT program said they would try to serve him and find him some shelter for the night. Jacob asked Anthony about the money he made working for Job Starts.

"I don't know, I stayed at the hotel a couple of nights."

"Why would you stay at a hotel when you have a free bed at the mission?" asked Jacob. He knew Anthony was lying because the Salvation Army had told him that he had come in every night.

"I had some friends come in from out of town and we hooked up," Anthony answered.

"Did you give your children's mothers any money?"

"Uh, no. I tried but they didn't want it."

Possible Approaches

Dealing with a homeless participant will be challenging for your program. He will probably have more issues than simply not having a place to live. Anthony had a substance abuse problem, a likely criminal record, and he lied to the staff. If a participant lies to the caseworker, it's hard to provide services of any kind because you can't trust him.

Contact Homeless Program

First of all, you need to find a homeless program for him to join. Many fatherhood programs don't have the training or experience to help him adequately. It's important for your caseworker to have many contacts throughout the community as Jacob did. He knew which shelters to call.

If your client is an ex-offender, refer him to a program that provides services to ex-offenders. In Virginia, we have a state-wide program called Virginia CARES which helps ex-offenders. They are well trained at placing people with a criminal history in jobs, finding housing, and even obtaining legal identification. It is important that you establish a relationship with any program that offers that service. It is a good opportunity to dual-enroll participants in your program as well as theirs. Remember that collaboration is extremely important to your success with your clients.

Another important avenue is to contact social services if the father is under 18 years of age. He is still a ward of the state, and they may not know that he is living on the streets. They should definitely be made aware of the situation, and they could also help him find placement elsewhere.

Find out if he truly is a father. Anthony came into the program out of desperation, and for all we know, he could be lying in order to receive help finding a job and a place to live. You probably can't provide services to young men who are not fathers because it could put undo pressure on your staff. There are other programs in the community that probably serve non-fathers better anyway.

Refer clients with a drug history to drug counseling.

He Must *Want* Help

Be aware of his actions and demeanor when he sits with you. Anthony's defiant attitude toward drug abstinence is a key sign that he may still be using drugs. Drugs got him into this situation, and he still sees nothing wrong with smoking weed. A certified drug counselor may help, but only if Anthony wants help.

Sadly, you may have to cut ties with a guy like Anthony. If a father of any background comes to your program and ignores the advice of the caseworkers, he will not succeed. We tell the fathers that if they follow our suggestions, they will be better off in six months, probably sooner. It will take patience and trust on behalf of the fathers as well as your staff.

If you don't think Anthony is buying into your program's philosophy, let him go. Make sure that you refer him elsewhere.

We always assume that each young man who comes into our program will do his best to straighten out his life and become an involved father. We can't succeed with everyone that comes in our door. However, we can be courteous, professional, and make a referral to another worthy program.

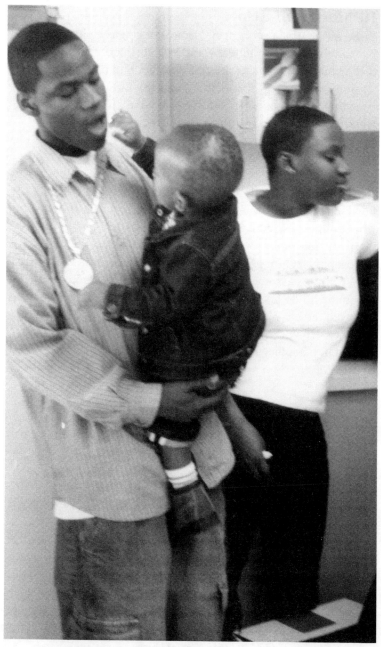

Jamie wants both of his parents to love and care for him.

9

Curtis — Baby's Mom Doesn't Want Him in His Child's Life

"I don't know where my mama's at. Ain't nobody been home since I got here," said Nicole. "You can wait if you want to."

"But you told me to be here at 6:00 to pick up Jamie," said Curtis. "How come every time I come to get him, he ain't never here?"

"Don't give me a hard time about it. I told you my mama's got him. If you don't like it, go back home."

Curtis walked back to his car ready to drive home. Before he turned the ignition, Nicole's mother pulled into the driveway. Curtis waited until they went into the house before he got out of his car. He went to the front porch but didn't knock because he didn't want another confrontation with Nicole. He had grown tired of the yelling that was directed at him every time he came to see his son. He waited on the porch for fifteen minutes.

"What's taking her so long?" he wondered. Anger building, he knocked on the door.

"Oh, so you decided to come back," Nicole said.

"I never left, you know that. I saw you looking out your window," Curtis yelled at her.

"I didn't know that was you. You could have knocked."

"Can you just get Jamie so we can go?" Curtis said. He was getting more and more frustrated, but tried to talk in a calm manner.

Nicole spent another fifteen minutes in the house. Curtis wasn't sure if she was dragging her feet on purpose or not. All he knew was it never took him that long to get his son ready when it was time to bring him back to his mother.

"You better have him home on Sunday at 5:00 like the judge said," Nicole ordered.

"Well, it's after 6:00 now and I'm supposed to get him at 5:00. I just might bring him back a little late," Curtis replied, challenging her.

"If you do, you won't get him the next time." Nicole always seemed to give him this trouble when it was his turn to get Jamie. He had asked his mom to come and pick him up, but she wouldn't do that. She said Jamie was his son, not hers. Nicole finally brought Jamie out at 6:20, almost an hour and a half later than he was supposed to get him.

"You better bring a new jacket for Jamie on Sunday," she said as they were leaving. Curtis didn't turn around and acknowledge her. He gave his son a kiss and hug, and buckled him in his car seat. As he pulled away from the house, he looked back, already dreading Sunday when he would have to take Jamie home.

Curtis and his son had become very close. He loved the weekends when they were able to be together. They did fun things like go to the park, zoo, museum, movies, and out to dinner. Jamie was three years old now, and was beginning to behave better out in public. Curtis cherished those moments, because that was the only chance he had to see his son. He never, ever went by Nicole's to see Jamie during the week. She gave him so much grief every other weekend that he didn't want to subject himself to the same treatment during the week. Curtis thought he would be even closer to his son if he could spend more time with him.

They had a good weekend. On Friday, Curtis took Jamie to a family cookout. Curtis' family loved Jamie, and attempted to spoil him as often as they could. On Saturday morning, they watched cartoons together. Saturday afternoon was spent at the park. Saturday night, they were at Curtis' girlfriend's house. Janeane thought the world of Jamie as well, and had candy for him whenever Curtis brought him over. Sunday morning they went to church together. Sunday afternoon was spent watching football and wrestling in the living room. Curtis couldn't believe how fast the time went by.

The time was now 4:30, and Curtis gathered up Jamie's clothes and toys. He looked at his watch, 4:35. "Huh, I knew it didn't take 15 minutes to get his stuff together," he said to himself. Curtis drove as slowly as he could without getting the other drivers angry with him. He despised taking Jamie home for two reasons. First of all, he missed his son very much when they were apart. Secondly, he resented Nicole. He knew she would have something to say; she always did.

Nicole was sitting on the porch when Curtis pulled up. They got out of the car and Curtis carried Jamie in his arms toward the house.

"Look, Mama," Jamie said as he stretched his arm out.

"What is that, candy? Where did you get that?" she asked. She didn't like Curtis giving him candy. She thought it made Jamie hyper.

"Janeane gave it to me," Jamie said.

"Oh no," Curtis thought. "Here we go."

"Janeane? I thought I told you to keep that tramp away from my son," she yelled as she took Jamie out of Curtis' arms.

"She's my girlfriend, and I can take my son where I please. He's my son, too," Curtis said.

"Well you won't be taking him anywhere if he's going to be around her," she said as she stormed into the house.

Curtis stood in the front yard expecting her to come back, but she didn't. He couldn't believe she was trippin' over this. Curtis had been with Janeane for two years. He never said anything about the guys Nicole brought around the house. As a matter of fact, he didn't even ask her about them.

Curtis walked back to the car feeling angry and sad at the same time. He was tired of putting up with everything that

Nicole put him through, and sad that he would not get to see or talk to his son for two more weeks. He thought about giving up, not coming back. That would be easier for everyone. But he had made a promise to himself that he was not going to put his son through the same experience he had gone through with his father. He wasn't sure how he felt now.

As he drove home he decided to skip his next visit. Nicole wouldn't mind if he didn't show up, and besides, Jamie probably wouldn't be there at 5:00 anyway. He would just make it easier on everyone. He thought about the great weekend he had spent with his son.

"It would be a lot different if it wasn't for her."

Possible Approaches

Many young fathers experience relationships like the one Curtis and Nicole have. The ROAD program always opens up the support group meetings with a "What's happening?" This is a chance to let everyone catch up on what is going on with the participants. The subject of the baby's mother (also called "baby mama-drama") and the bad blood between the two parents comes up more than any other topic. Many times we spend the session talking about how to deal with the baby's mother, and suggesting alternatives that the fathers can try.

We know the mothers are not the only ones at fault. In some situations, the father does not follow through on his promises. He may say he will buy some diapers, but doesn't. He may say he will give her money, but doesn't. He may say he will call her, but doesn't. If a father makes it a common practice to break promises to the baby's mother, she will resent him and take her feelings out on him whenever the ball is in her court (such as when he comes to pick up his child).

Her Feelings Toward Fathers in General

The baby's mother may have grown up without a father. She may harbor ill feelings toward all men because of the way she was treated by her dad. Dr. Wade Horn, Alice Feinstein, and Jeffery Rosenberg discuss the importance of father-daughter relationships in their book, *The New Father Book* (1998: Meredith Publishing Company, page 9). "The first relationship your daughter will ever have with a man is with you. If she loves and feels loved by you, she'll grow up feeling worthy and deserving of love. When she is older and begins dating, she will likely seek out boyfriends who show the same kind of love she received from you, her father."

If a young girl grows up in a fatherless home, and she hears how terrible her father is or how he is no good, it could, in fact, make her believe this is the way a relationship should be. She may feel she is supposed to talk bad about her child's father and be as unfriendly as she can be to him. To her, this may be normal behavior.

We asked a class of teenage mothers, "How many of you have grown up in a home without a father?" Out of 17 teenage mothers, 14 raised their hands.

Next question, "How many of you can raise a child on your own?" Every teenage mother raised her hand.

After we gave them information suggesting that a child is better off with a mother *and* father in his/her life, they became extremely animated with their defense. We realized children become what they learn. Many teen moms "learn" that they can raise a child alone because their mother did, and it is extremely difficult to persuade them otherwise.

Counseling Couple Together

The first step in helping Curtis is to sit down with him in a private setting. You need to find out as much about their relationship as possible. Does he break promises? Does he provoke Nicole? Does he treat her, at times, the same way he is treated? Curtis will be more honest with you in a one-on-one meeting than he will be in a group setting.

If you find he has broken promises and provoked her, you need to get him to realize that may be the reason she treats him so badly. Encourage him to be more pleasant and cordial. After all, she is the mother of his child, and he will have some form of relationship with her at least until the child turns 18.

Sometimes, a young father's friends pressure him into negative behavior. Advise him not to give in. Remind him that the friend is not the one who has to deal with Nicole or raise his child.

Another approach you might take is to speak to them as a couple. She may not go for this in the beginning. Nicole may feel that she is being ganged up on by you and Curtis. You may have to meet her and let her know that your true interest is in the well-being of their child. Let her know that is why Curtis is in your program, to benefit the child. You may also ask a female counselor to join you (like someone from Resource Mothers or another teen mother outreach worker) to even the playing field. She may feel less intimidated if there is a woman in her corner.

If she still refuses to meet with you, ask if her mother can attend the meeting. This can be a scary situation for Curtis as well as the educator. As one of our ROAD participants put it, "Moms don't play," which means they can sometimes get angry and abrasive. However, if Curtis is willing to talk with Nicole and/or her mother, he's indicating his willingness, for the sake of their son, to work toward better communication with Nicole. In such a meeting, he may be able to help them understand his sincere and intense desire to spend time with his son.

If a group counseling session doesn't work, you need to keep reminding Curtis that his child is the important thing, not how he feels when Nicole treats him bad. Remind him that being a father is not always easy, and being there for his son will be worth all the strife he has to endure. Remind him that Jamie's future success depends greatly on his involvement with his father.

In the support group, the participants will offer some great advice on how to deal with a difficult mother.

"Don't let it get to you. She's just trying to get to you. Don't let her ruin it," was a response from a dad in our support group. Sometimes, fathers just need to know they are not alone.

Practice Communication Skills

Perhaps you can also help Curtis learn better ways of communicating with Nicole. Even better, work toward offering both Curtis and Nicole tips on communicating with each other. Discuss the importance of I-messages, feed-back, and the problems sometimes caused by giving mixed messages. Perhaps their concern for their child's welfare will encourage them to be a bit more civil to each other.

Suggest that Curtis and his girlfriend not offer candy to Jamie, since Jamie's mother thinks it's bad for him. (Children do much better without many sweets.) Instead, perhaps he and his girlfriend will focus on activities with Jamie like coloring or playing ball. And of course a hug is always better than a piece of candy!

Some non-custodial dads feel they have to spoil their kids, but that isn't the case. Kids just want their dads.

Also suggest Curtis not skip that next visit with Jamie. Jamie needs him!

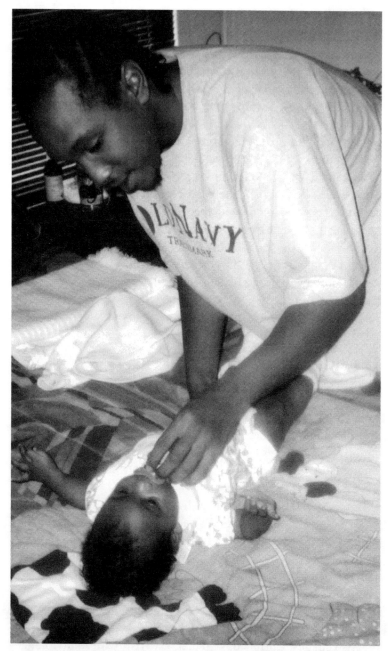

Suddenly Bobby was responsible for caring for and nurturing his son.

10

Bobby — Mom Says, "It's Your Turn to Parent Full-Time"

Bobby's phone rang for the fourth time. He was hoping whoever was calling would hang up, but the phone rang a fifth time. On the sixth ring, he picked up. "Hello," he said in a groggy voice.

"I can't do this anymore," she said.

"Can't do what?"

"I can't take care of our son anymore. I'm tired of doing everything by myself."

Bobby breathed deeply, trying to grasp the situation. "How are you gonna call me at 6 in the morning and give me this crap? Besides, you don't even know if I'm the father."

Kathy was speechless and furious. She knew that he was the father. Bobby and his mom, Ms. Johnson, came to the hospital and even brought a gift. She saw the look in Bobby's eyes when he held his son, and Bobby had visited Cody several times since his birth.

"Bobby, that's not fair," she said.

"I know it's not," he snapped back. "So what do you want me to do?"

"I want you to take the baby for a little while. Just until I get things settled down."

"WHAT? You want me to take the baby? I don't know
nothing about taking care of a baby."

Kathy was pleading, "Bobby, you're good with Cody and
your mom loves him. She'll be glad to have him in the house."

Bobby sat in silence, holding his head. This was too much for
him to take in, especially at 6 a.m. He knew his mom would
help, and he would love to see Cody more, but the thought of
helping Kathy out, after what she did to him, did not sit well.
After a couple of minutes had passed, he said, "Let me ask Mom,
but only for a week or so."

"Thanks, Bobby, I'll be there in ten minutes," Kathy said.

"Ten minutes?"

Ms. Johnson came home from work at her usual time, 3:15
p.m. Bobby had been there with Cody all day, and he held up
fine. He did not want to call his mom at work because she got in
trouble with her boss for receiving personal calls. Cody was
sleeping in his daddy's arms while Bobby watched reruns of the
Sopranos, his normal routine since he received his GED.

"What's my baby doing here?" Ms. Johnson asked. She
always called Cody her baby. She was wearing a big smile. He
was glad she was in a good mood, but Cody always put her in a
good mood.

"He's staying here," Bobby said.

"Staying here? For how long?"

"I don't know." Bobby filled his mom in on all the details.
She took it fairly well. She even seemed kind of happy.

"I just want you to know that you're taking care of that baby,"
she said. "I've already raised my four kids. I don't plan on
raising any more."

Bobby had been referred to the ROAD Program when the
baby was born. He said he would come to the meetings, but he
never showed up. Rick, the ROAD caseworker, knew Bobby
from playing basketball at the YMCA. Bobby liked Rick, but he
wasn't ready to join the program. He didn't feel he needed any
help.

Now Bobby's mom told him that he needed to get into the

program. He said he'd call the next morning.

Rick dropped by Bobby's house at 3:00 and had all the paperwork with him. He spent about 15 minutes going over the requirements and the benefits of the program. Bobby was receptive to everything Rick was telling him. It also helped that he already knew Rick. Rick started getting background information on Bobby for his file when Ms. Johnson walked through the door.

"Hey there, you must be Rick," Ms. Johnson said.

"Yes, ma'am, I'm with the fathers program," Rick replied. "Nice to meet you."

"Same here. So you gonna do something with my boy, here," she said as she pointed to Bobby.

"We're gonna try," Rick said as if he were amusing Ms. Johnson.

Rick wrote the information as fast as Bobby was giving it to him. Rick gave him some contacts for childcare, jobs, and employment training programs. Rick said he would make some calls for Bobby back at the office and give him a call with the information first thing in the morning.

"Well, he can't get jobs just anywhere," snapped Ms. Johnson. "He smokes that marijuana and they will drug test him, so you might as well find out where they test for that stuff."

Bobby made the appropriate calls and signed up for the job-training program at the employment center. The job-training program was divided into two parts: the classroom instruction, then on-the-job training. In order to move to the on-the-job training portion of the program, he had to attend fifteen days of classroom instruction. Once a participant completes his fifteen days of classroom time, he is paid minimum wage while he learns his chosen skill. After he completes the 20-day work-training requirement, the job-training program will help place him in a job earning a minimum $8.50 per hour.

The employment center was a great start, and they were extremely lenient with Bobby. His aunt watched Cody during the day so Bobby could get job training. He missed a day here and there, but they always let him come back to the class. They were understanding about Bobby having custody (at least for now) of his child. The teachers at the center would even call Rick and let him know when Bobby was absent.

After nearly three weeks into the program, Rick received a call that let him know Bobby had missed two days of class in a row. Rick dropped by Bobby's house to see what was going on. Rick heard Ms. Johnson yelling for Bobby to pick up the baby. Rick knocked.

"Come in," yelled Ms. Johnson.

Rick walked in and saw Bobby walking down the hallway with the baby. Rick said hello to everyone and asked Bobby why he had missed class for the last couple of days.

"The baby's been sick and my sister can't keep him when he's sick," Ms. Johnson interrupted.

Rick tried to talk to Bobby, but Ms. Johnson kept butting in and answering the questions for Bobby. Rick had noticed this in the past but didn't think too much of it. Ms. Johnson complained that if Bobby didn't find a job to pay for diapers and a babysitter, she was going to kick him out of the house. "All he does is smoke that stuff and want to hang out with his friends."

Rick remembered a couple of weeks ago, Ms. Johnson was laughing that Bobby loved to smoke weed, and would do so particularly when Kathy would come and get the baby. This confused Rick. One minute she was chastising Bobby for smoking, and the next she was almost condoning his smoking. Rick documented this in Bobby's file.

The following week at support group, Rick asked the guys to raise their hands if they were employed. Eight of the participants raised their hand, but Bobby did not. Rick asked him why he didn't raise his hand.

"I had to drop out," Bobby said. " My mom made me quit so I could get a job."

"Didn't you only have a couple more days before you were going to get paid?"

"Yeah, but she said it wasn't bringing in no money, so now I'm unemployed again."

Possible Approaches

This is an extremely difficult situation. First of all, Bobby is the acting custodial father, at least for the time being. It is rare to have a custodial dad as young as Bobby. Also, he smokes marijuana, and this, of course, is detrimental not only to Bobby's success, but to the health of his baby as well. Ms. Johnson doesn't seem to be helping much either. She sends mixed messages not only to Bobby, but to Rick as well.

Drug Counseling First

The first step in helping Bobby is getting him involved in some drug counseling. This could be an uphill battle, but at the very minimum, he needs drug education. Many young people don't feel that marijuana is harmful. Teenagers may receive untrue information from their peers. It is often difficult to educate young people about the dangers of marijuana and other drugs because the message from friends may carry more weight than what you may say.

Bobby needs to understand what all drugs, particularly marijuana, will do to his body. He needs to know of the harmful effects it could have on his son. Bobby also needs to be made aware of the negative impact drug use will have on his career. Many employers today drug test all applicants. If a job candidate has no marketable skills and little education, he is at a disadvantage. His job prospects are limited. They will be even more limited if he chooses to use drugs.

Teach Parenting Skills *Now*

Of all your clients, learning now about parenting a baby is crucial for Bobby. Even if he has Cody full-time only temporarily, he needs to learn parenting skills, and quickly. Right now, being in charge of Cody may be a little frightening for Bobby. Remind him this is a wonderful time to bond with Cody and form a relationship that will continue even if Cody moves back with his mother.

It's especially important that Bobby become knowledgeable about parenting — knowing more about babies his son's age will help him be a better father. Also important, this is a factor in finding joy in parenting along with the work involved.

Grandparent Support Group Needed

It's important to talk with Bobby's mother, or better yet, get her involved in a grandparent support group. It may prove extremely difficult to talk to her one-on-one about Bobby's situation. You are an outsider. You didn't help raise her family. Ms. Johnson may feel you are accusing her of being a bad parent. This is a delicate situation, because if you offend her, she may withdraw her son from your program.

A support group could be a great help not only to Bobby, but also for his mom. Many localities offer a grandparents' support group. If you do not have such a group available, consider starting one for the families of your program's participants.

Once their child is going to be a parent, many grandparents-to-be get overprotective. Not only can this hurt the new parents, but it ultimately harms the new baby as well. Many grandparents want their sons to get a job, any job. The basic theory is good, but if a young father doesn't work on his education or "hard" job skills, his future will definitely be compromised, as will his child's.

Grandparents usually drive home the message of child support. This is great, but young dads need to build relationships with their babies as well. If a young dad has a healthy relationship with his child, he will be more inclined to work and pay child support. Fathers of any age don't want to be seen simply as a money machine.

Parents of teen moms tend to be extremely overprotective, at least at first. I've heard many grandparents tell their daughters, "If you want our help, you will break up with that boy" (the father). The young mothers are caught between the proverbial rock and a hard place. If she stays with her child's father, she betrays her family and may have no place to live. If she chooses her parents, she pushes the father out of his child's life.

I've seen many court cases involving our participants when they were faced with similar situations. The mother's parents don't want to consider the child's best interest; they want to pursue revenge against this young man for getting their little girl pregnant.

The support group will help the new grandparents understand the vital role they play in their grandchild's life. They can learn more about the support the new parents need, and how to help the young parents become independent as soon as possible.

Ms. Johnson seemed to enable Bobby's drug use; Bobby is receiving mixed messages on this issue. Just like teen parents, grandparents may need a support network to realize they are not going through this alone. Information can be shared among the grandparents on coping mechanisms, ideas for success, and ways to include both parents in the raising of their child.

For more information on the grandparents' role when their teenager has a child, see *Teen Parents and Their Parents: Managing Three-Generation Living When Mom or Dad Is a Teen* by Jeanne Warren Lindsay (2003: Morning Glory Press). Included are comments from grandparents who are part of a support group along with suggestions for developing such a group.

Limited Employment Opportunities

Bobby must also realize that he is limited in employment opportunities. The father support group is a great place for interaction among the participants. They are likely to encourage Bobby to make responsible choices about his future.

Bring in an employment specialist to talk about careers. Be sure to include a vast array of available jobs such as construction, computers, food industry, etc. Get information concerning the average pay for jobs with companies that offer drug screening versus those that do not. Take Bobby to job fairs or employment expositions. Many employers attend these fairs, and Bobby may see something that peaks his interest.

If you have the resources available, hook Bobby up with a mentor or someone he can job shadow. This may prove difficult because it takes effort on behalf of the mentor. However, it could be invaluable for Bobby to see a positive man working hard in the banking industry or some other field.

The downside, as with any participant, is you may not be successful getting Bobby on the right "ROAD," despite all your efforts. Don't get discouraged. Persist, persist, persist! Give Bobby the responsibility of making the phone calls, setting up the interviews, and following up. Give him the leads and as many pointers as you can, but don't allow him to get too dependent on you to get a job for him.

Praise Bobby for his efforts at every opportunity possible. Be positive and don't dwell on any setbacks he may encounter. Always keep the focus on his child, not his employment. As long as we focus on the positive involvement and support that fathers give to their children, everything else will eventually fall into place.

11

Demetrius — His Daughter Lives in Another State

Demetrius had been driving several hours and he was exhausted. The drive itself wasn't that bad, but making the trip was always tough after working from early morning until mid-afternoon. When he had a good night's sleep, the six-hour drive was easy as pie. The reason he was driving, though, made the trip worthwhile. He was driving to see his daughter, Savannah. Savannah was his joy, his only child, and his baby girl. He was madly in love with her. He hated the fact that she lived so far away. He was only able to make the trip about every two months. But this time, he had a surprise for her.

Demetrius worked at a local restaurant. He had worked there for three years and he was moving up the corporate ladder. He started out as a dishwasher. His manager thought he was too friendly to be stuck doing dishes every night so he asked him to be a waiter. Demetrius made good money with his tips. The customers loved him because he never wrote anything down. He kept all the orders in his head. He once received a $100 tip from a table of business executives who were impressed that their waiter could remember the drinks, appetizers, salads, entrées, and desserts for a table of twelve.

Demetrius moved from waiting tables to cooking. The general manager was impressed with Demetrius' flexibility in the restaurant, so impressed, he promoted him to kitchen manager. The demands on the job are tremendous. He often works ten-hour days, six days a week. Weekends off are a rarity in the restaurant business, but whenever he has one off, he makes the six-hour drive to Philadelphia to see Savannah.

As Demetrius approached Philadelphia, he started to get angry at Michelle, Savannah's mother. They first met at the restaurant. Michelle was in college and came in with a group of her sorority sisters. Demetrius waited on her table and Michelle was smitten immediately. Demetrius' smooth demeanor and rapport with people attracted her, and she loved a man in dreadlocks.

Michelle started frequenting the restaurant on a regular basis, and soon asked Demetrius to a party on campus. That night, the two ended up in Michelle's dorm room drunk with passion. Two weeks later, she told him that she had missed her period. Demetrius wanted to be supportive, but Michelle's parents were furious. They demanded Michelle come home so they could watch her and help with the baby. Michelle didn't even finish the semester.

Michelle's parents tried their hardest to keep Demetrius away. They would cleverly schedule trips when Demetrius was to be in town. Often when he arrived, he had to wait outside the house for hours because they had gone out to dinner or on some errand. They frequently came home so late that Savannah was asleep.

Michelle was stuck. She was living with her parents and had to live by their rules. She still cared for Demetrius but her parents gave her the ultimatum: dump him or you are on your own. Whenever Demetrius called to check on Savannah, he and Michelle always had pleasant conversation. He didn't think he loved her, but he thought of her as a friend.

Demetrius thought of the many confrontations he had with the parents. They would berate him in front of Savannah, and Demetrius would fight back. He tried not to, but he could only take so much. He was tired of being pushed around and forced out of his daughter's life.

Demetrius finally arrived at 307 Maple Avenue. Once again, no one was home. While in the car, he wondered why he tried so hard when everyone wanted him to stay away. Why did he have to work so desperately to be involved in his child's life? Maybe for Michelle's parents, the problem was the fact that their blond haired, blue eyed daughter got involved with a dark skinned guy with dreadlocks.

Living in the suburbs of Philly, a white girl wasn't often seen with a black guy. The fact they had a child together probably reminded Michelle's father every day. Demetrius wasn't a deadbeat dad, the kind often reported in the news. He wanted to pay child support, but they would take nothing from him. He wanted to establish paternity, but Michelle wouldn't sign the forms. He wanted his daughter to come to Virginia to spend a weekend or longer with him, but the family said that would never happen. He missed her first words and her first steps. He was miserable.

"Thank God for the fathers program," he thought. The fathers program in Virginia had helped him understand the importance of staying as involved as possible and maintaining a civil relationship with Michelle no matter how her father treated him. The group understood everything that he was going through, all of his frustrations and pain. If it weren't for the group, he'd have given up long ago.

At 8:30 p.m., Michelle's SUV pulled into the driveway. Demetrius got out of the car and waited for the family to emerge. He saw Savannah in the seat and saw that she was awake. That made him happy. "Daddy," she said, pointing to her father.

"He's not your daddy, Savannah," said Michelle's father. But Savannah ignored him and ran to her daddy. Demetrius scooped her up and hugged her tightly. Tears started streaming down his face.

"You just won't stay away, will you?" asked Michelle's father. Michelle dared not say a word in Demetrius' defense.

"No sir," answered Demetrius. "As a matter of fact, I'm moving here to be with my little girl."

Michelle's father stormed into the house, but Michelle stayed outside with her daughter. "How are you going to move here? You don't know anybody," said Michelle.

Demetrius couldn't stop smiling. "My counselor in the fatherhood program back home got me in touch with a program up here. Mr. Gregory told them my situation, and they said they would look out for me. I have a meeting in the morning with some guy named Doug Dowel. He's going to help me get an apartment and find a job in a restaurant."

Michelle started smiling, too. "That's terrific, Demetrius. Now Savannah can see you anytime she wants."

"Well, it's still going to take about a month or so until I can move up here. But I'll be coming almost every weekend to get everything straight." Demetrius kissed Savannah and gave her a hug. He handed her to Michelle and said, "I better go check into my hotel. I don't want to be late for my meeting in the morning. I'll be here at 11 o'clock to pick up Savannah, okay?"

Before Michelle could speak, Savannah said, "Okay, Daddy, we'll go to Chuck E. Cheese!"

"Okay, pumpkin, we'll go to Chuck E. Cheese!"

Possible Approaches

This is an extremely tough situation for Demetrius and everyone involved. It could also be difficult for you to handle. Most programs are not equipped to handle situations like this.

Many fathers like Demetrius may come to your program seeking only assistance in becoming more involved in their daughter's life. Many fathers have come into the Fatherhood and Families office at TAP seeking a specific service. A father may come in wanting a job (the most common request), needing a lawyer, or seeking to get a child support order explained or even reversed.

The Fatherhood and Families program has the policy that all fathers must become enrolled to receive services. Participants must become involved in all aspects of the program to receive any of the benefits of the program, and that means attending support groups and employment counseling. However, this policy can be, and often is, flexible.

If a father like Demetrius has a fantastic work history, he may not need to participate in the employment counseling and the soft-skills job classes. Whatever your policy may be, leave a little freedom to bend the rules. For a father like Demetrius, we would definitely make an exception.

Contacting Fatherhood Programs in Other Areas

Offer Demetrius the full benefits of the program. He may want to get involved to the fullest extent. Whether he wants the total program experience or not, you can offer him some support. Call a fatherhood program that is located in Philadelphia (or wherever your participant's child may live).

Don't panic if you are not familiar with programs in other states or cities. You can call the National Fatherhood Initiative or NPCL (National Center for Strategic Nonprofit Planning and Community Leadership). See appendix for contact information. They can help you find a suitable program in another area.

If the particular state has a Statewide Fatherhood Campaign, you may contact them as well. Some states with established statewide programs are Virginia, Pennsylvania, and Texas.

Inform them of your participant's situation and ask for their assistance and advice. They may be able to help you concerning the laws in that locality.

Finding Legal Help

You also need to get Demetrius in touch with a good family law attorney. Inquire about Demetrius' financial situation and his ability to pay for legal counsel. If he needs assistance, contact Legal Aid. Legal Aid will determine if the case is appropriate. If they reject him, do your best to get him an attorney for free. I personally don't give "our" attorney's name to fathers who aren't enrolled, but I would make an exception in this case. If Demetrius is able to pay, definitely acquire the attorney that provides free services to your program. This will be a good way to pay back the lawyer who has helped you in times past.

Encourage Demetrius to enroll in a parenting class immed-iately, one that focuses on his child's current age. After he moves, perhaps he and Michelle can enroll in a class together. When the two parents agree on child rearing practices and discipline strategies, their child benefits.

In this situation, Demetrius was extremely happy that he had enrolled in the support group of the fathers program. He was able to learn that respecting his child's mother was important. He was able to understand the important part he had to play in his child's life. The support he received from the group gave him the strength he needed to make the drive to Philadelphia so often.

The Virginia program helped him get involved with a fatherhood program in Philadelphia in order to help him relocate. The program also helped him understand the importance of living there (in the same city) to be as fully involved as he wanted to be. The fathers program gave him the courage and the resources to move in order to be closer to his daughter.

12

Allen — Released on Probation And He Needs a Job

Allen sat nervously on the hard bench. He tried thinking about other things like basketball or Katie, his girlfriend.

"What is taking so long?" he thought.

He'd been sitting on that bench for over an hour. The four others with him had already gone in, and all four returned. Some had tears in their eyes, others had a blank stare. Seeing those guys come back to the hard bench made his stomach turn more than the long wait. He had been here before but had never seen every guy return to the bench. Now, everyone was waiting on Allen's name to be called, waiting for the van ride back to Coyner Springs Juvenile Detention Center. The silence was broken by the sound of keys turning the lock of the steel door.

"Smith, time to go," the bailiff called. Allen stood and lifted his hands to the cop so he could remove the handcuffs. Allen hated the handcuffs. They always clamped them on his wrists as if he were a rabid animal. Once the cuffs were off, he rubbed his wrists to get the blood circulating again. He never complained because it did no good.

The bailiff grabbed Allen by the arm and led him into the courtroom. The judge looked busy reading. "Probably my file,"

Allen thought. The bailiff led him to the table on the other side of the courtroom. At the other table was a lawyer. "Preppy punk," Allen said to himself. His probation officer sat in a seat directly behind the lawyer.

Allen turned around and saw his mom. She gave him a smile and whispered, "Hi, baby." Katie was sitting beside her with his son, Frankie. She had gained some weight since last month. She looked like she would give birth to his daughter any day.

"Mr. Smith, good to see you this morning. I hope we didn't keep you waiting long," the judge said.

"No, sir. Not too long," Allen replied. The judge sounded in a good mood. But that didn't matter because he'd already sent Allen's cellmates back to the bench to wait for the van ride back.

"Mr. Smith, we are here to review your case and determine whether or not we should release you back to your family," the judge said. "Mr. Myers, you may go first."

"Thank you, your Honor," the lawyer replied. "Mr. Smith was charged and convicted on malicious wounding charges and drug possession in January. He has spent only four months in jail. Before the January incident, he had been arrested for drug possession and driving without an operator's license. For both of those charges, he spent a total of three weeks in jail. We feel he has not learned his lesson, and if he's released, the Common-wealth fears he will soon end up back in jail. So at this time, we request that he be detained in Coyner Springs for at least two more months."

Allen was hot, but he continued to look at the judge. The counselors at Coyner Springs had told him to look at the judge and remain calm at all times.

"Thank you, Mr. Myers," replied the judge. The judge shifted his attention toward Allen's probation officer. "Mr. Merchant, what do you have for me?"

"Thank you, your Honor." Mr. Merchant stood as he talked to Judge Stone. "Allen Smith has been incarcerated for the last four months and has been a model prisoner. He has earned extra phone privileges every week but two since January. On my visits with him, he has never seemed angry or belligerent. We've talked about the steps he needs to take to be successful once he is released. He currently owes $473 in restitution. He plans on paying that as soon as possible. He is the father of a son and also has another child on the way. He has expressed interest in being with the baby's mother in the delivery room. The baby is due next month.

"I would like to request the court that Mr. Smith be released to his mother and remain on probation for three years with weekly drug tests. As a condition to his probation, I request that the court order him to enroll in the ROAD program. They will help him find a job, obtain his GED, and he will have to attend parenting classes. If he violates any conditions of his probation, a violation order will be issued and we will pick him up."

Allen appreciated Mr. Merchant's court testimony. He had always gotten along with Mr. Merchant. Mr. Merchant was tough, but he gave his probates the benefit of the doubt if they were trying to do well. Allen had some friends who had probation officers who were always putting them down rather than helping them improve their situations. While Allen sat wondering what would happen, he thought of the talks he and Mr. Merchant had in the past. Allen really wanted to do well for him. He hated that he had put himself in a situation that got him locked up again.

"Mr. Smith," the judge bellowed, "would you like to say anything?"

"Yes, sir." Allen rose to his feet. "Mr. Merchant told me 'If you keep doing what you always done, you keep gettin' what you always got.' I want to have a chance to prove to him that I'm not going to do what I used to do. I want to prove to my mom that she did a good job raising me, and I want to prove to my kids that their father ain't no failure."

Allen sat down feeling a little sick in his stomach. He didn't know what to think. The Commonwealth attorney sure didn't want to give him a chance. Allen looked at the judge while he shuffled his papers and wrote notes on his file.

"Mr. Smith, I've heard the statements made by Mr. Myers and I tend to agree with him. Not only did you have a malicious

wounding charge, but you also had drugs on your person. I
appreciate the statement given by your probation officer, Mr.
Merchant, and I also feel good about what he said. Young man,
you are lucky to have him as not only a probation officer, but he
seems to be mentoring you as well.

"Now the question is, are you going to listen to him, or do
your own thing? Your statement was taken by this court with
some caution. Have you learned a lesson from this? I don't
know. Were you serious about what you said? I truly hope so. I
see here in your file that your father is currently incarcerated. Is
that correct?"

"Yes, sir."

"What's your relationship like with your dad?"

"I don't have a relationship with my dad."

"Well, your kids deserve a relationship with their dad. It is my
hope that you turn your life around, if for no other reason but for
your children. Kids need both parents, and that doesn't mean
only occasionally.

"You will remain on probation, and I will add one more year
to that. You must maintain weekly contact with Mr. Merchant
and take drug tests weekly. You must also complete forty hours
of community service, and I am ordering you to enroll and
actively participate in the fathers program. I will order a review
for two months from today. I will expect to see some improvement in your situation by then. Good luck, and I don't want to
see you in this courtroom for any reason other than your review.
Do you understand?"

"Yes, sir."

Possible Approaches

Allen needs immediate services for him to become successful. Many young men who are released from incarceration or boot camp don't get the proper attention they need when they are sent back into their community. Probation officers can only do so much. Most have a large caseload; their job is to send their probates back if they violate the terms of their probation. They may tell the ex-offenders what direction they need to take, but they are too overwhelmed to give intensive services. This is where your program is vital to Allen's success.

We recently had a father come into the office a week removed from incarceration. It was his third time being incarcerated, and he came out motivated to change his previous behaviors and situation, not only for himself, but also for the sake of his three children. He enrolled in the program, but left feeling he did not need what we had to offer.

Two weeks went by and we heard nothing from him. He finally showed up at a support group meeting. It's the Fatherhood and Families program policy that all fathers who enroll in the program must attend a support group meeting and a soft-skills job class before they can begin receiving services. During the first half of the support group meeting, he was extremely reserved and didn't participate very much. Slowly, he began to talk and get into the dialogue of the group.

After group was over, he approached me and shook my hand. "I really enjoyed this," he said. "I'm definitely going to be back."

This father had never experienced this type of open support group before. He had been in anger management classes, but our group was a different experience for him. Men talking about their struggles and expressing their love for their kids was new to him and he enjoyed that. Because of his experience that night, he became extremely involved in all aspects of the program.

Immediate Employment Is Crucial

The first week of any ex-offender's release is extremely important. If he has no job possibilities or opportunities to locate employment, he may resort to other ways, perhaps illegal, of making money. The Center for Employment Opportunities (CEO), located in New York, serves ex-offenders and offers programs and job training opportunities upon their release. They work with the state probation and parole board to determine the release dates of incarcerated men and women. They are highly successful at putting ex-offenders to work and providing them with career options, rather than just any job.

One of the keys to CEO's success is enrolling clients within one week of their release. This gives several options to the ex-offender. CEO can put their clients to work within a day of enrollment. One thing an ex-offender does not need is idle time.

Once you get the phone call from Mr. Merchant, you need to make a phone contact with Allen. After you get your initial information, make an appointment for a home visit. Give him several options for available jobs for which he could apply. Give him all the information about the father's program. This will give him a chance to read about your organization and share with his mother and girlfriend.

Also make an appointment with him to visit your office and get acquainted with the staff. It's important that you build the relationship with him and make him feel comfortable with you. It may help to have a joint meeting with Allen and Mr. Merchant, especially since Allen likes and trusts Mr. Merchant.

Applying — With a Record

Before you take Allen out to look for a job, help him complete his application. Many employers are not open to hiring ex-offenders. Some organizations may require that they not hire anyone with a criminal record due to the nature of the job. Others simply don't trust applicants with a record. This may be discrimination, but it is rarely challenged.

It is extremely important that Allen be truthful about his rap sheet, because he could get fired if the truth should come to light at a later time. He would be fired immediately, even if he were an outstanding worker. An application is an official document; therefore the applicant must be truthful about everything in the document.

Companies ask different questions related to an applicant's criminal past, and applications may include questions concerning criminal history. These questions may be asked in different ways:

1) Have you ever been convicted of a felony?

2) Have you ever been in jail?

3) Have you ever been arrested?

It is important for the applicant to know the difference between the three questions so he can answer the question directly and completely. If the question on the application is, "Have you ever been incarcerated?" and the applicant lists his convictions, he is not answering the question. It is possible to have been convicted of a crime and not to have been incarcerated.

Another way to answer the questions honestly is to write, "Yes, would like to discuss in the interview." This will give the applicant an opportunity to talk about his criminal past and, more importantly, give the potential employer a sense that he is really making an effort to turn his life around. But if he doesn't write down the offense, this can come back to haunt him.

Debbie Mukamal, a staff attorney at the Legal Action Center in New York City, suggests that for some clients it might be useful for caseworkers to help clients draft an explanation of their criminal history. Put it on a separate sheet of paper that can be attached to their job applications. This strategy of answering the question directly but providing additional information will give clients more room to explain their conviction(s), as well as an opportunity to discuss the positive changes they have made in their lives since being convicted. In the section of the application asking whether they have ever been convicted, Ms. Mukamal advises that clients answer, "Yes, see attachment."

Employment Specialist Can Help

An employment specialist should be brought into the picture as well. Allen needs employment quickly, but he doesn't need a dead end job that he will tire of in a matter of weeks. If Allen remains unemployed, he may distance himself from the group because he feels he is not receiving adequate help. An employment specialist can help him consider his preferences of workplaces and, with your assistance, locate possible avenues for him to explore.

The employment specialist may also get Allen enrolled in a job training program or classes at a local community college. With the added training, he will be more marketable to potential employers. A great place to receive invaluable information regarding employment issues for ex-offenders is Public/Private Ventures in Philadelphia, PA. Their website is <www.ppv.org>

Allen also needs to get involved in the support groups as soon as possible. He will get encouragement from the other fathers enrolled in the program. A positive relationship with you is vital for him to succeed. The fathers that feel the connection with you or your staff will work harder because they know if they stumble, they have you to help them up again.

Allen has built a strong relationship with Mr. Merchant, and he needs to have that mirrored with your program. Relationships are crucial in not only recruiting potential participants, but more importantly, keeping the fathers involved and helping them work toward their goals.

13

Roman — They're Taking His Children Away

Roman was absolutely heartbroken. His children were going to be placed for adoption and no one was helping him. The Department of Social Services was characterizing him as a no-good, deadbeat, worthless excuse for a father. Roman felt he had done everything DSS and the court had asked him to do, but it wasn't good enough. They labeled him "angry" and unfit to care for his children. They felt he couldn't give his children the environment they needed or deserved.

Roman heard about the fatherhood program and wanted to see what they were about. He had walked by the offices of the program many times on his way to court or to his supervised visits with his children, but never gave much thought to going inside. A caseworker with the Head Start program told him he should go down and talk to the counselors at the fatherhood program. Roman, on the advice of the caseworker, called the office and made an appointment.

Dale, a counselor with the program, greeted Roman at the door and escorted him to his office. As they sat down, Dale asked, "Roman, how can I help you?"

"I want my kids back."

Roman began to tell the story of how his kids had been taken from him. He was at work one night, on the graveyard shift, when his wife called him in panic. "They took our babies," she screamed. Roman raced home from work to find his children gone.

"What happened, Denise?" Roman asked. He was getting angry.

"I just stepped out for a minute and when I got home, the people were taking the kids with them," she replied. She was crying and shaking.

"Where did you go? You know you're supposed to stay home!"

"I had to go to the store and get some milk."

"At one o'clock in the morning?" Roman was pacing and furious. He felt like punching the wall.

Roman finished telling Dale the story and how he had to go to supervised visitation. DSS also wanted him to take anger management classes and a psychological evaluation. Dale told him that he would help him and get him enrolled in the program. Dale invited Roman to support group that night, and Roman agreed to come.

Possible Approaches

After Roman left the office, Dale called DSS and asked to speak to Ms. Clark, the caseworker assigned to work with Roman and his wife. Ms. Clark informed Dale that she could not talk about the case because of confidentiality. Dale offered to fax a release of information form signed by Roman.

Ms. Clark called after she received the fax. She told Dale a lot of information that Roman didn't give. Roman had lost two other children about five years earlier in another city. The reason those children were taken from the home was neglect and an unclean living environment.

Ms. Clark went on to tell Dale that Roman always waits until the last minute to complete the requirements DSS has put on him. She also told him that Roman had been locked up and released last week on a malicious wounding charge. Denise had a history of drug abuse with no signs of stopping. There were also incidents of domestic violence between the couple.

"Is there any chance that he can get his children back?" asked Dale.

"No chance," answered Ms. Clark. "The process is already in motion and the court hearing is in two weeks. That is when their parental rights will be taken away for good. Besides, he is a very angry man and displays his anger every time he comes near me."

"We Can't Help You"

Roman came to the office at 5:30, about thirty minutes early for the support group. Dale asked Roman to come in the office so they could talk about his conversation with Ms. Clark.

"Roman, there is nothing we can do for you," said Dale.

"What do you mean, you can't do nothing for me?" asked Roman.

"I talked to Ms. Clark from DSS today and she told me about your past. We have no clout. The judge isn't going to give you your kids back just because we go in there and tell them that you deserve them. It doesn't work that way."

"My past is my past and it should have nothing to do with this case," said Roman.

"How come you didn't tell me about your other children that were taken away from you?"

"That wasn't our fault. The social workers said because our house was a little dirty that it was not fit for children. It wasn't unfit."

Dale asked, "What about your wife's drug abuse?"

"That ain't got a thing to do with me. I don't even live with my wife anymore."

"What about the malicious wounding charge?" Dale continued.

Roman rolled his eyes and threw up his hands. "That wasn't my fault. This guy that knows my wife was talking junk to me and I tried to leave. He was telling me I wasn't a man and calling me a punk. I tried to do the right thing by leaving, but he kept following me, then he pushed me, so I hit him. What am I supposed to do, let him hit me?"

"What about the domestic violence charge?" continued Dale.

"I come home from work and my wife has some people over. I'm tired and I want to take a nap so I ask them to leave. They don't want to leave, so I ask 'em again to get out of my house. Then, one of my wife's friends jumps on my back and my wife comes and tries to help her. They biting me and hitting me, so I hit her back but only to get her off me. Next thing I know the cops are at the house and I'm going to jail again."

Dale was rubbing his temples. "Roman, Ms. Clark tells me that you are very angry and show that anger toward her."

"Dale, she lying. I ain't never showed her no anger. She always talking down on me like I ain't worth nothing. I go in the office and it's all white ladies and they look at me like I'm there to rob them or something. I'm passionate about my kids. Can't a grown man get passionate about his own kids?"

"You seem angry right now," said Dale.

"I'm mad because ya'll supposed to help me. Ain't this a fathers program? I'm a father and you don't want to help me!"

"All We Can Do Is Try"

Roman was crying. Dale felt for him. It took Roman's display of anger and passion to remind Dale of what he did for a living.

"Look, Roman. I don't know if we can help you or not. DSS said that the wheels are already in motion. Like I said, I don't know if we can do anything, but we will try. All we can do, though, is enroll you in the support group and help you with the requirements that DSS wants from you."

"Alright," answered Roman. He was still crying.

"I want you to know that we may not even get to speak on your behalf in court. All we can do if we get the opportunity is to let them know what you've done since you've been in our program. I can't tell them that you deserve another chance because we don't know you that well. All I can do is tell them what we know. I want you to get as involved in the program as you can. Is that all right?"

"Yeah, that'll work," replied Roman. He was still crying.

"Come to group next week. I don't think you would be comfortable in there tonight, but make sure you see me before the week is over, okay?"

During the next two weeks, Roman came into the office almost on a daily basis. The ROAD Program helped him get his anger management counseling sessions, set him up with the job developer, and involved him in the support groups. Roman was faithful in his attendance.

Roman arrived at the office at 8:45 a.m. for court. Dale grabbed Roman's participant file and the two headed to court.

The judge wasted no time. He immediately took the parental rights away from Denise. She had failed to comply with her drug treatment program, and DSS informed the court of her sporadic involvement at the supervised visits. It didn't look good for Roman.

The judge looked at Roman and asked what he would like to say. Roman pointed to Dale and told the judge that he had a witness from the fatherhood program.

The judge responded, "I know this young man," as he pointed to Dale.

Roman told the judge how he had been wronged and how much he loved his kids. Roman said he had left his wife and all he cared about was getting his kids back. Then Roman asked the judge if Dale could say some words. The judge agreed.

After Dale was sworn to tell the truth, he took his seat on the witness stand. The judge asked about Roman's involvement; Dale told him exactly what Roman had done since he had enrolled. Dale frequently looked at Roman's progress notes so he wouldn't leave any detail untold. After the judge questioned Dale, the DSS attorney asked if they could ask some questions. The judge conceded.

The DDS attorney asked Dale, "Do you know that he has a criminal history and a recent malicious wounding charge?"

"Yes, ma'am, we are aware of that," answered Dale.

"Then why would you offer a man like this services?"

"Because he's a father," replied Dale. "We help any father who wants our services."

Roman Gets a Reprieve

The judge was ready to rule. "Mr. Sparks, I want to commend you on getting involved in this program. I've worked with many of their clients and am impressed with what they have to offer. But that isn't going to get you completely off the hook. I want you to continue in the anger management classes and I want you to take another psychological evaluation. You must attend all aspects of the fatherhood program, and they will let me know if you don't comply. You still have to work with DSS on the supervised visitation. I'll give you two months to see improvement, and we'll see where we can go from there. I also want DSS and the fatherhood program to have close and frequent contact with each other to monitor your progress. Mr. Sparks, the only reason I'm giving you a chance is because you are trying to improve your situation. I want you to listen to Dale and the staff at the fatherhood program and do everything they tell you. Are we understood?"

"Yes, your Honor." Roman was crying, this time with tears of joy.

Part II

Developing Your Program

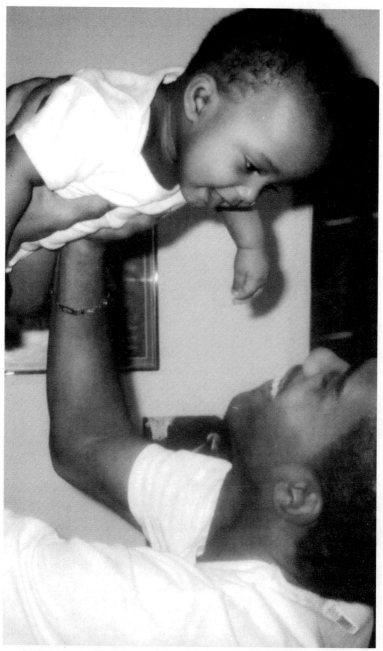

Is there a need for services for young fathers in your community?

14

Plan *Before* You Start

Pre-program planning is essential. This was one of many problems the ROAD program experienced. At first we did not plan. We knew we wanted to "Reach Out to Adolescent Dads," so we jumped into it without the necessary background work. Take the time to do some research. The better prepared you are, the greater the chance your program will be successful within a reasonable time.

Is There a Need?

First, determine if your community has a need for such a program. Researching local teen pregnancy statistics is a good place to start. Every state keeps a record of teenage births. Roanoke City has a high teen pregnancy rate compared to the state average. The number of teen births has decreased in recent years; however, our rate still is almost double compared with other localities in the state.

Start by going to <www.childtrends.org> and clicking on "Facts at a Glance" for current statistics on teen pregnancy, You'll find such information as the number of teen pregnancies in each state and in many of the larger cities in the United States.

While it is true that most teen mothers give birth to babies fathered by men over 20, there are still many teenage fathers who need your help.

Most states do not compile statistics on fathers. In reality, some fathers are hard to pin down. Welfare reform may change that, since it requires mothers who apply for welfare to list the name of the child's father. In the future, statistics may be collected to account for the fathers.

You could also conduct a confidential survey, but this may be difficult. It is hard to conduct a mass survey that will be accessible to many teen males. School is a good place to conduct these surveys, but most school systems will shy away from a survey containing sexual content. (Many schools feel that a survey asking about sexual history will persuade or encourage teenagers to engage in sexual intercourse.)

Surveys are also very time consuming. If you have the staff and the manpower to conduct one, it may be a great tool to assess the need for the program.

If surveys give you some shocking data (such as a high number of teenage fathers or a high amount of drug use), you may be able to use the local media to help you gain support for establishing a teen father program. Stress that you will be trying to correct negative behavior and foster responsibility in young fathers.

Defining Your Target Population

After you can show that your locality needs a teen father program, define your target population. The ROAD program officially offers services to fathers aged 13 – 25, but we have an open door policy that allows a father of any age to come to the support groups.

We have found that many low income fathers over the age of 30 have the same issues that younger fathers experience (employment, child support, education). Although our target population is for young fathers ages 13-25, we will never turn away a father.

Establishing Goals, Expected Outcomes

Goal-setting is extremely important for your program as well as your participants. The ROAD program did not do this in the beginning, and we paid for it dearly. We knew we wanted to assist young fathers, but we didn't know exactly what we wanted to do for them. This is also important for evaluation purposes. Sit down with your staff and discuss what you expect of young fathers. You may want to ask some of your participants as well.

Keep in mind that you can change or add to your program goals. You may decide through trial and error that a certain goal is not what the program should focus on, or you may want to add a goal along the way. Goal-setting is a continuous process of revising and fine-tuning.

When you bring a new dad into the program, let him know the program goals. If he doesn't know what is expected of him, he is far less likely to reach his goals. The ROAD program keeps a list of the goals in each participant's folder. There is also space for the father to include additional personal goals. (See pages 182-183, Appendix.)

The ROAD program goals and objectives are:

1. No father will cause a repeat pregnancy until he is emotionally and financially ready for another child.

2. Each father will establish paternity.

3. Each father will contribute child support.

4. Each father will obtain and sustain legal employment.

5. Each father will become more involved in the life of his child.

Your program goals may be different from the ROAD program, and that's okay. Your program should address the needs of *your* participants.

Identifying Services

What will you provide for the program? Providing services is necessary to reach your goals and have your fathers succeed. You cannot give them their goals and send them on their way, hoping that they do what they are supposed to do. You have to be beside them and ready to support them.

We provide job counseling and health services (because of our collaboration with the Roanoke City Health Department). We also provide job training programs, child support intervention, parenting education, and mediation counseling services. Now that we are a member of TAP's family, we have access to great services for ex-offenders (VA CARES), childcare assistance (Early Head Start and Head Start), employment training (This Valley Works Center for Employment Training), and even assistance for homeless families (Transitional Living Center).

The ROAD program has incorporated some co-parenting classes and may include a mother's support group as well. We found that when we talked to the father about respecting his child's mother, and putting the child's interest first, that it did no good unless the mom also received that message. ROAD now seeks to work with the entire family instead of just one parent.

An important service that just about every program should offer as needed is transportation. Many young men can not get a job because of lack of transportation. The ROAD program provides transportation to interviews and work. We also provide bus passes if they need them. You may only need to do this until they get situated in their job, and can afford their own bus passes or vehicles. Don't let them take advantage of you.

ROAD lets each father know that we will give them a ride to work if they give us enough advance notice. If someone calls ten minutes before their shift begins, we may not be available. Once, for an entire week, I took a young father to work at 5 a.m. You may not want to take it to that extreme, but be as flexible as you can.

Don't list services you can't provide because that would damage your program's credibility. If you don't come through for these fathers when you say you will, you may lose them. For the services you cannot provide, find other programs to help you.

One of the best things to happen to ROAD was a lawyer, Jimmy Robinson, an attorney, whose work with us is described on pages 60-61.

Jimmy provides services for our program at no charge. He also speaks to our fathers as a group on occasion and lets them know their paternal rights. His energy and dedication to our fathers and the ROAD program has not only helped our fathers, but also helped our program's image in the community as well.

If you can get a lawyer to be a legal advisor for your program, do it. It may take a while (it took ROAD four years to find Jimmy), but it's worth the time and effort.

Collaborating with Other Programs

"It's not about you or us, it's about them." Lee Pusha, Fathers at Work employment coordinator, says this often. What he means is that we sometimes have to remove our egos and our hang-ups about working with other organizations. Sometimes, one organization will not work with another because they don't like them, they want all the power, or want all the recognition. These petty differences can hurt an organization's efforts to provide the best services to their clients. One of the most important things you can do for your program is to collaborate with other groups and organizations.

Collaboration is wonderful because it means more services for your program and less work for you and your staff. Contact various organizations and discuss what you can do and provide for each other. A young father may come to you and need legal advice. Unless you have a law degree hanging on your office wall, find a legal organization, firm, or private lawyer that is willing to provide legal advice for your clients.

Employment is another area where you may want to collaborate. Locate job-training programs and utilize their services. They are often free and they will benefit from the added attendance your young men provide. Both you and your client will benefit from the training.

You may also collaborate with employers. ROAD has a cooperative agreement with Crystal Spring Linen Service of Roanoke. They offer employment, when available, to our fathers who are unemployed. They provide full-time positions (with benefits) as well as part-time jobs. The only thing required of

ROAD is weekly phone contact or a visit with the owner to update her on our participants who are employed by her company. We are also encouraged to visit our young dads at the factory. With a partnership like this, we are better able to serve our fathers and provide support when needed.

You'd be wise to use the educational networks in your community. A young father may want to acquire a GED (General Educational Development). If you have a relationship with the programs and community colleges that provide GED education and testing, a phone call informing them of your client's wishes may be all you need to do.

Many programs make the mistake of trying to do everything on their own with little or no community support. The ROAD program was guilty of this for a time. It simply makes things more difficult for you and your staff. Besides, with more collaboration, your clients will be better served, and getting grant awards will be easier. Foundations generally prefer to offer grants to programs that work with other organizations.

Developing Your Budget

When compiling a budget, include rent, utilities, salaries and fringe benefits, staff development and educational supplies, plus food, transportation, and other incentives for clients. The ROAD program offers incentive prizes to the young fathers that partici- pate in the support groups. T-shirts, shorts, hats, gift certificates, and CDs used to be given for regular attendance. We now give the fathers baby clothes, toys, and books for their children.

At every support group meeting, we have food. Pizza, chicken, hot dogs, potato chips, cake, and sodas are provided for the participants. Young men need to eat, and this may be what attracts them to the program initially. If it is, that's okay, as long as they attend.

An annual Father's Day cookout is also held, as well as a banquet for each of the fathers who graduate from the program. (Usual time for a father to be in the support group is six months.) All of these things cost money, and a lot of it.

Finding money is not an easy thing. Be as precise as you can, but make sure you budget enough for the services you will provide. You don't want to cut your program short because you did not budget enough money. In fact, money is probably the biggest hurdle you face when starting your program or struggling to maintain it. You need money to do your job and provide services.

The ROAD program has been plagued with budget concerns from the beginning. I wish I had a magic formula for you, but I don't. Apply for as many grants as you can. Seek donations from private companies and businesses. Ask them to sponsor an event or outing for the dads and their families. Also go to fraternities and other men's organizations to ask for donations for your program.

Ask for in-kind contributions from other organizations. In-kind contributions could be cost of mailings, computers, printing services, phone services, etc. This can take some of the burden off your program and will improve your standing when you apply for grants.

Utilizing Volunteers

Volunteers are a great way to expand your program without taking a chunk out of your budget. The hardest part is finding a volunteer with the available time and the needed enthusiasm. Volunteers may be able to help you with transportation or programming activities. Look for organizations, such as the Junior League, to donate items like refreshments for your group meetings or baby clothes. Find some local churches or fraternal organizations to provide mentors. Mentoring will not require a lot of time, and will set a positive example for your young fathers.

You may not need a volunteer to help you on a regular basis. Enlist the help of people who will be available when you need them. An example would be someone to help you with a cookout or to accompany you on a group outing. Churches are wonderful places to look for good volunteers.

We are lucky to have a model volunteer in the ROAD Program. Loralea Buffington is a nutrition assistant for WIC

(Women, Infants, and Children Food Program) and is always
there to help us out. She approached us about ROAD and told us
she wanted to get involved. Loralea looks out for funding
sources for us, helps us get food for the support groups at a
minimal cost, helps prepare food, and attends the support group
and offers insight to the fathers.

Help from Other Teen Father Programs

Try to find other programs like yours or the one you are
building. They can give you advice on their program that may
help you with yours. You've probably heard the phrase, "Don't
reinvent the wheel." It may sound corny and cliché, but it's true.
Use what other programs deem successful, whether it is services
they provide or evaluation methods they use. It may save you a
lot of time and energy.

Ask them about things that do not work and failures they may
have encountered. Ask if they can send you any material. I have
not found a program that refused to share their experiences. The
ROAD program is more than happy to share information with
programs across the country.

Probably the best way to accomplish this is to surf the net.
The Internet is full of information on fatherhood programs.
NPCL (National Center for Strategic Nonprofit Planning and
Community Leadership), the National Fatherhood Initiative, and
the Virginia Fatherhood Campaign are great places to start your
search. Contact information for these groups is included in the
Appendix, page 192. They can put you in touch with other
fatherhood programs. You may call these organizations and
request information on programs to contact. You can also access
the ROAD program at <www.roadprogram.org>

Evaluating Your Program

Evaluation is extremely important for several reasons. The
first is that positive evaluation will prove that you are doing a
good job, and that your fathers are doing a good job. Everyone
loves positive feedback.

The second reason is that negative evaluation will show that you need to change some things. It does not necessarily mean you are doing bad work or your fathers are not succeeding. It may simply mean that you must change your approach.

If you receive a negative evaluation, don't throw in the towel. Sit down with your staff or supervisor and attempt to find alternative ways to meet your goals. For example, we found that after some poorly attended meetings, the staff was not conducting home visits, as they should have been.

We took this information to the staff and let them know that home visits are a vital part of building the relationship with the participants. Once the home visits increased, so did the support group attendance.

The third reason evaluation is important is money. When you apply for grants and can prove that your program is working, potential foundations or other funding sources will be more willing to give you their money. Foundations do not give away money to programs that are not successful. Also, if you have an evaluation process in place before you start your program, foundations will be more inclined to give you a chance.

The ROAD program is evaluated partly on self-report. We take the word of our participants regarding their progress. However, we also talk to employers, check court documents, and interview the child's mother. If the fathers reach their goals, we document this information in their file. At the end of the program we compile and calculate the data received, and hope for a good evaluation.

We also keep a program diary. If a father has a success or failure, we document that in his file. Sometimes numbers do not tell the whole story. Remember that you are working to help the father, not to reach a certain percentage of clients who attain a specific goal. If you take that approach and work with each individual in your program, the numbers will take care of themselves.

A focus group can be another evaluation tool. The ROAD program utilizes the staff of the Roanoke Teen Pregnancy Prevention Project (TPPP) to conduct these sessions. TPPP asks the young men questions such as:

1. What do you like about the program? Dislike?

2. Do you like the ROAD staff? What do you dislike about them?

3. What do you like about the support groups? What do you dislike?

4. Do you feel the ROAD program has helped you in any way?

5. If you could change anything about the program, what would it be?

If you are organizing a focus group, make sure you leave the room during the evaluation sessions. You don't want them to make kind remarks about you simply because you are in the room with them.

You may also use participant feedback forms. (See Appendix, p. 191.) This feedback can be beneficial to you and for your evaluation. Who better to tell you if you are doing a good job than the participants themselves? Our fathers recently told us that they wanted the moms to be included in some of our activities, so we incorporated some "family nights" into our sessions.

Evaluation takes time, time you'd probably rather spend providing services to your clients. However, in the long run, being able to provide those services will depend at least partially on the results of program evaluation. It's an important part of providing services.

15

Hiring Your Staff

Perhaps one of the most difficult tasks a program director has is to hire competent and caring staff. It's difficult to look at resume after resume to determine who would best fit your program and, more importantly, who would best serve the interests of the fathers you will be serving. I've talked to many directors who have a great staff, and as a result, their program flourishes. Every good program needs a good director, but it is the staff, the people who are in the field and serving your fathers on a daily basis, that will make your program successful.

Reflecting Client Population

Your staff needs to be a reflection of the clients you serve. They should also have some background in the field or some experience. College degrees may not matter when dealing with young dads. Some of the best people you could have working for your organization may be men who were young fathers themselves. The number one thing you need is people who can relate with your clientele. You can have a person with a BA and all the certifications you can find, but if they can't relate to your clients, the education is no good. We have a young man who graduated from our program and continues to help out at support groups. As soon as possible we'll add him to our paid staff.

If you have only women working in your fatherhood program, you will find it hard to reach young dads. Women may be able to provide effective services and they may be very committed to the program as well as to the fathers. But a staff of only women cannot effectively model appropriate fatherhood for young men. Young men need to hear from older men, those that have been there, done that. Having men on your staff is important.

The same rule applies to racial, ethnic, and religious identities of your participants. If a majority of your population are Hispanic fathers, but you have a staff of all white persons, then your chance to be most effective decreases.

Fathers of all nationalities and races need to see successful men to whom they can relate, and this may begin with the racial makeup of the staff. This does not mean that you cannot be effective with participants who are of a different race than you, but it can definitely be a put-off to young fathers coming into your program.

The Fatherhood and Families Program, which houses ROAD, has managed to hire a diverse staff that reflects the population of our participants — three African American men, one African American woman, one white woman, and one white man. We also have an ordained Baptist minister and a Muslim imam on board. Our staff works together in harmony and relates well with one another as well as with our participants.

If you're in an area with many Hispanics, you'll want to include Hispanic bilingual staff. You will also need to collaborate with an ESL (English as a Second Language) program.

Whatever the ethnic makeup of your community, attempt to mirror that makeup as much as possible.

Checking on Qualifications

Reviewing resumes is a tedious task, and after twenty or more applications, they can begin to look remarkably alike. The first thing to look at is experience. Sometimes a program sets educational requirements such as a Bachelor's degree or

Associates degree for all staff members. It's better to be flexible. Don't discard applicants simply because they lack the academic credentials. Experience is vital to the success of your case workers because performance on related jobs will carry over to your program. Any experience in working with young men is usually an advantage.

There are, however, some related experiences that can be detrimental to what you are trying to accomplish. Once a man applied for the position of fatherhood case manager in our organization. He had more than twenty years experience working with young men in the juvenile justice system. He had been a probation officer, surveillance officer, and earlier in his career, he was a police officer. His experience working with young men appeared to be what we needed. I asked him a question about how he would deal with a young man who did not want to pay child support.

"I would tell him to pay, and if he doesn't, I'd call my friends downtown and tell them to lock him up," he yelled as he banged his fist on the table in front of him. "If that doesn't scare him, I'll go to court myself and seek an order against him." Needless to say, he disqualified himself from the position very quickly.

Interviewing Applicants

After you have narrowed your list of acceptable applicants, it is time for the interview. Look for more than qualifications during the interview, because if they didn't have the qualifications, they wouldn't have made it this far in your hiring process. The interaction between you, the applicant, and the panel (which I prefer), is how you will guage their effectiveness in communication and perhaps their passion for the job.

We once interviewed two women for a part-time position with the program. Applicant A had a Bachelor's degree, was highly skilled in working with our population, and extremely organized. Applicant B had more hands-on experience working with young men, but didn't have a Bachelor's degree. During the interviews, applicant A impressed us with her management skills and attention to detail. Applicant B blew us away with her charm and interpersonal skills.

Applicant B was able to project to the panel her passion and her desire to work with young fathers and their families. The panel didn't get the same feeling about applicant A. This in no way diminishes the qualifications of applicant A. She would have been great in an administrative position with our program, but applicant B seemed more personable for our population.

We hired applicant B, the first woman we hired in our program. Some of us think she is the best person for the program. In fact, she is now the full-time coordinator for ROAD.

Organizational Ability Is a Must

Applicants should be proficient in case management, good time managers, and very organized. It is imperative that detailed records are kept on all of the fathers enrolled in your program.

Each caseworker may have twenty to thirty participants at any given time. With court cases, doctor appointments, child visitation, job interviews, apartment hunting, and other needs of the participants, time management skills are crucial.

Your staff must also accurately and articulately report every contact and even attemped contact with their clients. This will be beneficial for court appearances if the need arises.

The results of your intervention with young fathers, whether positive or negative, need to be documented. It is vital that you keep track of each individual's progress. For each participant who comes into your program, compile a file for his information.

Filing Information

The ROAD program used to keep all of our participants' information in a manila file folder, but we began accumulating so much information, it became tedious to locate documents easily. You will have assessment forms, goal sheets, court documents, referral forms, release of information forms, and the very important client contact reports, all of which must be kept together for each client.

We now use six clip case management folders. These provide plenty of space to keep important information and makes organizing all of our data easier. And organization is a must for case managers.

Our documents are separated as follows:

Section 1   Referral forms and release of information forms
Section 2   Intake forms
Section 3   Assessment forms (Use two forms, one for his
             personal habits and one for his fathering habits.
             Include typed evaluations on his progress.)
Section 4   Goal sheets and update sheets
Section 5   Client contact reports (Document every
             encounter with each client, whether by phone or
             in person.)
Section 6   Court documents and miscellaneous (Include
             activity sheets utilized in group sessions.)

Another tool our staff uses is tape recorders. We often have three or four fathers in the office waiting for various appointments with our staff. You don't want to keep fathers waiting, but you need to be organized and document all information from the meeting and the contacts. After the meeting, our case managers talk into the recorder and communicate everything that was done in that meeting. They then proceed to talk to the next waiting father. Once there is a break in the day, they document the information in the participant's files. This is particularly effective when you are doing home visits or run into a father on the street.

Of course each father's file is confidential. It is important to keep detailed, documented files for each participant. A good quote to remember when documenting is, "If it's not written down, it didn't happen." The more orderly your files are kept, the easier it will be to report your results. Don't worry about having too much information in the files. It is better to have more information than not to have enough.

See the Appendix or contact the ROAD program for copies of the forms we use.

Educating Yourself and Your Staff

The more you know about fatherhood, the better equipped you will be to serve your target population. As already mentioned, the Internet is a great place to get information, but the information you receive there is often limited.

One of the best places to start is your local bookstore. Find as many books on fatherhood as you can. The National Fatherhood Initiative (NFI) offers a resource catalog where you can obtain books on this subject. In addition, some of the proceeds go to help NFI continue to reach communities and promote the importance of fatherhood.

Some wonderful books that the ROAD program has used for education are:

- *The New Father Book* by Wade F. Horn, Alice Feinstein, and Jeffery Rosenburg (1998: Meredith Books)
- *Fatherless America* by David Blankenhorn (1996: Harperperennial Library)
- *Father Facts* by Wade F. Horn, Ph.D. (2002: The National Fatherhood Initiative)
- *Father's Rights* by Jeffery M. Leving, et al. (1998: Basic Books)
- *Throwaway Dads* by Ross D. Parke and Armin A. Brott. (1999: Houghton Mifflin Company)
- *Child Custody Made Simple* by Webster Watnik (1999: Single Parent Press)
- *Teen Dads: Rights, Responsibilities and Joys* by Jeanne Warren Lindsay (2001: Morning Glory Press)

See the Appendix for other books that can help educate you and your staff.

Attend conferences and workshops that focus on fatherhood whenever possible. Conferences are a great way to gather ideas from other programs. It is always beneficial to network with other programs because they may be able to offer support to you and your program.

The National Center for Strategic Nonprofit Planning and Community Leadership (NPCL) offers great workshops that can help get your program started or offer you additional ideas if your program is already established. You will be educated by perhaps the best facilitator in the country, Pam Wilson, who also co-wrote the Fatherhood Development curriculum. You may contact them at <www.npcl.org>

16

Choosing and Evaluating a Curriculum

A curriculum is absolutely essential because it will give you lesson plans and topics that are important for educating your fathers. The ROAD program had no curriculum in the beginning, and we were often scrambling to find interesting topics to discuss with the participants. Topics such as child support, legal issues, childcare, etc. are important, but if you limit your discussion to those areas, you are not focusing on the total person.

Helping young men become better fathers involves helping them become better men first. Self-esteem issues need to be addressed as well as job training, education, sexuality, discrimination, and even their own personal feelings about their father.

Choosing a curriculum can be a trying and time-consuming chore and most people don't know where to start.

Must Fit *Your* Population

First of all, the curriculum must fit the needs and the population of your program. Is your program in a rural, urban, or suburban setting? Are a majority of your participants white, African American, Hispanic, Asian, or other backgrounds? What are the goals of your program? Economic stability, paternal involvement, ex-offender services? You need to answer these questions before you seek a curriculum. It would be disappointing to buy a curriculum and not have it fit the population or the needs of your program.

You may choose curriculum which offers training so you can utilize the curriculum to its fullest capacity. A curriculum will also provide activities that you can use to get your points across to your clients.

The best curriculum we've found is *Fatherhood Development: A Curriculum for Young Fathers.* Dr. Jeffery Johnson and Pamela Wilson compiled and designed this curriculum. It can be obtained only by attending one of the NPCL (National Center for Strategic Nonprofit Planning and Community Leadership) workshops. The ROAD program has been using their curriculum since 1997.

NPCL offers an exceptional three-day training to educate participants on the many facets of group facilitation and the contents of the curriculum. They also offer specific trainings for your program's needs. They can tailor their trainings to accommodate your program.

NPCL's curriculum is great for fathers who live in urban areas. Activities are included that portray real life situations for young fathers. Many of the chapters and activities are suitable for fathers of any ethnic group and any location. The curriculum was actually compiled for the Public/Private Ventures Young Unwed Fathers Project. The Young Unwed Fathers Project focused on fatherhood programs in several urban settings across the country.

If you work with a largely Hispanic population, a good place to begin your search is California. Jerry Tello, president of The National Latino Fatherhood and Family Institute in Los Angeles is an excellent resource. Mr. Tello's program also deals, with great success, with gang activity in the Latino community. Héctor Sánchez-Flores, Center for Reproductive Health Research and Policy, School of Medicine, University of Caliornia, San Francisco, is another invaluable resource who has worked successfully with a Hispanic population.

Unique Needs of Rural Program

I have not found a good curriculum for rural fathers. Programs for rural fathers face many challenges. Public transportation is non-existent in rural communities. Approaches to reach dads may need to be different. For example, the Rockingham Community Action Board of Lexington, VA, often visits fire stations to talk and reach out to other fathers. Many of the men in the community simply hang out or volunteer at the fire department. This is highly successful in Lexington because the program is going to where the fathers are.

The Lexington program also has fishing tournaments and hunting trips for the fathers and their children. Hunting and fishing are a tradition in many rural settings, and this is a bonding time for these fathers and children.

Ron Clark, director of the Virginia Fatherhood Campaign, once said, "Instead of serving the 'Boys in the 'Hood,' they serve the 'Boys in the Woods.'" The program in Lexington is a great example of molding a program to fit the needs of the community. A curriculum tailored for inner-city fathers probably would not be suitable here.

If you are looking for curriculum, contact NPCL or the National Fatherhood Initiative for curriculum information. You may also contact your state fatherhood campaign or other fatherhood programs near your area. The Internet is a great place to search. Don't try to write a curriculum for your program if you don't have to. The program in Lexington may have to do that because not much is available concerning rural fathers

It's very time-consuming to put together a quality curriculum, however. Generally that time could better be used recruiting clients and providing services to them.

Parenting Curriculum

Many fatherhood programs tend to neglect parenting classes, mostly because they focus on employment. Good dads, after all, need to work to support their children. They need to pay child support. Society tells us that fathers need to be providers. This is as true now as it was 100 years ago. But it's time to take fatherhood to the next level.

Focus on employment and child support among other issues, but fathers are also needed as nurturers. They need to be involved, loving, influential parts of their children's lives. They need to change diapers, prepare meals, and even fix their daughter's hair. But how do fathers gain this knowledge? They are often left out of the "mommy stuff." Fathers need to be viewed as more than the disciplinarian and the provider.

All fatherhood programs need to focus on the involvement part of a dad's relationship with his child. For the fatherhood movement to be fully effective, we must push dads to be involved in all aspects of their children's lives. Programs should place a priority on parenting skills.

A court of law may suggest or require that specific fathers go through parenting skills classes. Is your program ready for this challenge? In many support groups for fathers, issues tend to center around the struggles fathers go through in order to be good dads. This needs to take place, but more needs to be included in the dialogue.

The *Fatherhood Development* curriculum that the ROAD program uses for its support group offers some of the parenting skills that fathers need. Effective discipline, how children learn through play, and how fathers can establish trust are sessions the curriculum addresses. This is a great start, but you will want to add more how-to-parent content to your program. Nutrition is an area that needs to be addressed. Children need to eat good food. Often, non-custodial dads give their children junk food, like candy and soda. Non-custodial dads, of course, are not the only ones; many parents are guilty of this practice. If you don't already address this in your group, ask a nutritionist to come to your program and give a presentation on good nutrition.

Child development needs to be discussed. Give fathers a chance to understand the different stages of development their children are going through so they know how to communicate with and discipline (teach) their children.

Some localities offer parenting classes on a regular basis. This could be a good partnership for your program and theirs. If you can use their expertise and incorporate their curriculum in your classes, your fathers will get the best of both worlds.

If you don't have that option, find suitable material for your program and for your participants. Among the many areas to address in a parenting class are:

- Infant care
- Baby-proofing your home
- Nutrition
- Medical information
- How children learn
- Effective and appropriate discipline (Always remember that discipline means to teach, not to punish.)

One curriculum designed especially for teen fathers, and which focuses mostly on the art and skills of parenting, is *Teen Dads: Rights, Responsibilities and Joys* by Jeanne Warren Lindsay (2001: Morning Glory Press). It's a comprehensive guide to parenting from conception to age three of the child, and is appropriate for fathers, whatever their relationship, or lack thereof, with their child's mother. Relatively inexpensive, it includes reader-friendly books, workbooks, and a comprehensive curriculum guide. The guide includes lesson plans, handouts, and lots of activities, many focusing on father/child involvement. Teen dads are often quoted in the text to reinforce the parenting concepts presented.

Make parenting skills education a priority in your program. Not only do your fathers deserve it, but their children deserve fathers who are educated, sensitive, and emotionally attached to them.

What About Childcare?

Childcare is something you may never have to worry about in your support groups. Perhaps most of the fathers you work with will not be custodial fathers. The ROAD program provided support groups for years before the issue of childcare needed to be addressed.

Many programs are not equipped to provide childcare and

support groups at the same time. The ROAD program, in the early years, had only two employees; therefore we could not have someone be with the children while the others were facilitating the group.

When a father who was enrolled began coming to group with his daughter, we simply let her stay in the group. This was a great opportunity for the fathers to see a custodial father interact with his child. We had a great time with this father and his daughter in-group. She was only six months old and was very active. She would cry, eat, and sleep. He would bring bottles to the group to feed her. Diaper changes were a regular part of the group. We were able to go forward in the support group with little distraction.

A few weeks later, the trickle down effect came into play. More and more fathers started bringing their children to group. They saw the interaction that the first father had with his child, and perhaps saw the attention he was getting, so they wanted to include their children.

At one group, we had four children at the weekly meeting. One father played non-stop with his daughter and barely participated in the group discussion. The more children you have, the more the focus is on the children, and it can be difficult to hold the attention of your participants. This may be the time to provide childcare.

The ROAD program used to provide fatherhood support groups for Head Start. In exchange for the support groups and father-child outings, Head Start agreed to provide the refreshments for the program as well as the childcare for the meetings. Teachers and family service specialists with Head Start volunteered to provide the childcare, and Head Start gave the volunteers comp-time for their participation. Not only was it great to have free childcare, but it was provided by professionals who worked with children for a living.

If you need childcare for your program, seek outside agencies or volunteers within your organization to provide this service. Head Start is a good place to start. A great collaboration could be formed. Also, Head Start on a national level is becoming pro-fatherhood, and this will be another avenue for you and your program to explore, and perhaps expand your participant base.

Whomever you choose to partner with or provide childcare, make sure they are certified in infant-child CPR and first aid. Have toys and books available for the children. Ensure the service is provided, if needed, but also be certain it is a safe, clean, fun, and learning environment for your participants' children.

You might want to expand some of your group sessions to include a time for father/child interaction. Because children need and demand lots of attention from their parents, this usually needs to be separate from the regular group sessions. Very small programs with only a few participants may find it possible to include the children in the regular sessions. It's a great way to foster bonding between father and child.

Young dads, as well as teen moms, need special help.

17

Finding and Recruiting Young Dads

Now that you have done your homework, you're ready to go to work. You have educated yourself and your staff, listed goals and objectives, collaborated with other programs, and compiled a budget. You are now ready to take your program to the young fathers.

First, You Find Them

Probably the most important and difficult task you and your staff have is the actual recruitment of teenage fathers. Start off by contacting local teen mother support programs. Resource Mothers, Department of Social Services, schools, and other organizations that offer services for teen mothers are excellent places to contact. They already have the mothers in their program, and they can talk to the young ladies about getting the children's fathers involved. Perhaps you could be a guest speaker at one of their meetings.

Give everyone you contact some written information on your program so they can forward it to their clients. Most teen mother programs will welcome you and your services. Be prepared to handle some criticism or cynicism from the teen mothers if you speak to them yourself. Keep in mind that part of your job is to change the negative way some people feel about their child's father.

Contact juvenile probation and parole officers, school health clinics, guidance counselors, coaches, and after-school programs. Try to meet with each program or person individually. You will make a more lasting impression by meeting them in person than you will by sending a letter or placing a phone call.

Refer to "Outreach/Recruitment Strategies" on pages 175-176 for more tips on recruiting young fathers. Also see chapter 18, "Promoting Your Program."

Recruiting young fathers is one of the hardest parts of your job. Don't be disappointed if you get only a few commitments. Initially the ROAD program, during one recruiting phase, had a commitment rate of 36 percent. That's okay. Don't make the same mistake we did in the beginning. We were depressed that we didn't have all ten fathers instead of the three or four that did attend. If this happens to you, show the same enthusiasm with two fathers as you would have with twenty. Be concerned about the fathers who are there.

Meeting Face-to-Face

Once you get a list of names, it's time to make some phone calls. You will most likely receive positive responses over the phone. You will, however, occasionally hear someone say he isn't interested. Expect this reaction. Remember, this guy doesn't know you from Adam. When you receive a positive response, don't sit back and think the young fathers will start walking through the door. It's now that the hard part begins.

Schedule a face-to-face meeting if at all possible. You will have a higher caseload if you meet the fathers in person. A home visit is often best, but give your prospective client a choice of location for meeting. If you can't schedule a meeting within a few days of your phone call, send a follow-up letter immediately. Give the prospective participant some written information about your program.

When you meet him, you have to be a salesman. Your

program is your product. If you talk to him in a monotone and are not enthusiastic, don't expect him to be. Learning to communicate with young men takes time and practice. Don't try to be someone you are not. You've got to be genuine. If a young father thinks you are fake or phony, he will be turned off.

It is important to get some background information on the young men and let them know what services you offer. Tell them there is no risk involved. It costs nothing, and takes up little of their time.

Those All-Important Home Visits

Home visits are a valuable service that programs should provide if at all possible. Some fatherhood programs do not visit their clients in their homes, and sometimes there are valid reasons for this, particularly for programs in rural areas. Some of the rural programs have to travel as far as 30-45 miles one-way to reach a participant's home. A home visit in this case could take as much as three hours, and the mileage could have a huge impact on your budget.

Many young fathers lack transportation and find it difficult to come into your office to enroll in the program. By going to the participant's home, obtaining the information needed for enrollment purposes is easy and convenient. It also puts the participant at ease knowing that you are willing to come to them to offer services or help. This is crucial to building trust in your participants.

Regular home visits give you a chance to see how the participant is living. If a father is trying to get custody, his living environment can be a deciding factor in whether or not he gets custody or visitation. One of our fathers was involved in a visitation hearing. He had previously been awarded Saturday visits from 9 a.m. to 6 p.m., but he wanted his children to spend the weekend with him. During the hearing, the mother accused the father of having unsafe living conditions and objected to him having the weekend visitation.

When I took the stand, I was able to review my client contact notes and tell the judge that this young man's living environment was extremely stable. The only downfall was he didn't have beds for the children. The judge ordered the father to purchase two beds for his kids, and he would be awarded weekend visitation. The ROAD program was also able to find him some beds through community contacts for a lot less than he would have gotten them from a furniture store.

Sometimes the court appoints a guardian at litum to do a home visit to determine the living situation of the father. In such a situation, you can "pre-visit" and help the young father get his place in order before the court advocate or DSS officer comes to do their inspection. You are there to help the father, not to deceive the system. This will be beneficial for your father, and he will be more likely to take some advice or constructive criticism from you than from someone he doesn't know. Your program can also help him obtain furniture or other things he needs for his children.

Home visits are also important to keep in touch with your fathers if they are not attending support groups. He may not feel comfortable in the support group and he may need a little more personal attention in order to get acclimated to the program. The key to your program's success is not only the services that you can provide, but also the personal relationships with your fathers. You have to sell yourself as well as the program. Home visits are also beneficial if the father doesn't have a phone. The home visit may be the only way to keep in contact with him.

Try not to be "shockable" when you enter the home. I have entered homes that were unclean and almost unlivable. I once went into a home while a young man was cooking breakfast. He invited me into the kitchen and I saw a gun on the kitchen table. His son was sleeping in his room. After we made small talk, I asked him about the gun. We talked for about an hour, and he explained his need to have the gun. His lifestyle was such that he felt he needed it to protect himself. I asked him why it was on the table, and he replied that he always kept it close by.

After he told me his reasoning for carrying the gun, I talked to him about the dangers not only for him but for his family. I talked to him about the possibility of his son picking the gun up and firing it. An accident like that could kill someone or even himself. He agreed to be more careful and put the gun away. Over the next few weeks and several home visits, we continued to talk about the gun; I advocated for him to dispose of it. He finally conceded, and during many more home visits, I never saw the gun again.

I would not have seen the gun had I not performed a home visit. Not every father will give in and dispose of the gun, but this father did and his family is better for it. Home visits not only provide you a chance to establish a relationship with your client, but also observe his situation and make recommendations that will help him and his children.

Obtaining Background Information

You can get some background information before you even meet the father. The ROAD program distributes referral sheets to various programs. (See ROAD form on page 179.) When they have a young father to recommend, they put the information on paper and mail or fax us the referral sheet.

Information should include name, address, phone number, school of attendance, if any, how many children (born and/or unborn), the name of the child's mother, and space to make additional comments. This makes things much easier for all parties involved. Plus, you will come across much more strongly if you have some background information when you talk to the young father.

Keeping Them Interested

You have done your homework, recruited, and gotten some fathers who are interested in your program. Having the fathers stay involved, however, can be an exhausting experience. You and your staff must keep them interested and pleased with the services you provide. If they feel they are getting nothing out of the program, they will walk out.

Providing all the services you promised when you were recruiting is most important. If you don't come through on job training, transportation, legal advice, whatever you told them you would do, they will take you for a liar. The program's credibility could be ruined by not coming through for just one father. Remember that your most powerful marketing tools are your clients and former participants.

Foster a caring environment. It is important that you recruit staff who are genuinely interested in helping the young men. If you hire someone who is in it only for the money, it will have a detrimental effect on your program and its reputation. Have a staff that goes the extra mile. Be there for the fathers in any situation that they may encounter. The ROAD program staff carries pagers and gives each participant permission to beep us at any time, day or night. This will generate trust with the young men, probably the most important factor when dealing with teenagers.

You should also give them a sense of ownership of the program. Let them decide which topics they would like to discuss, what kind of food they would like at the meetings, and where they would like to go on special trips. Ask them for their opinions and seek feedback from the group. If they feel their opinions matter and that they have a vote in some of the activities, they will feel a sense of belonging. They will feel comfortable in the group and more often than not they will stay. Refer to "Retention Strategies" on page 177 for more helpful tips.

Value of Support Groups

Support group meetings can be the most effective forums for young fathers to share their feelings with other guys who are going through similar experiences. These meetings can be a time of bonding as well as education. Embrace them as they walk through the door, as well as when they leave. Invite them to share their experiences or ideas at any given time.

The support group should be interactive and laid back. You are a facilitator and not a teacher. A facilitator lets the group communicate with one another, and the communication is open for everyone to get involved.

Remember that they may have been in school or at work all day. Don't act as if you are trying to get the kids to learn the theory of relativity. In short, don't be boring. If you are boring, the guys will not be interacting and will not learn anything. Be positive and upbeat. If you are bored, the participants will be as well.

Have food available at every meeting. Even if your program can only afford potato chips and Kool-Aid, have something for them to eat. The ROAD program often has hot dogs, corndogs, and hamburgers, and the staff does the cooking. This can save you a lot of money.

Have a lesson plan and go over it with your staff. Be prepared to teach, but allow the group to interject at any time. If they want to talk about something other than what you have prepared, be flexible and go along with the group discussion. You can always go over your subject matter next week.

The ROAD program once had planned a lesson on interviewing and job skills. We begin each session by asking the fathers what has happened since we were last together. One of the fathers started talking about his baby's mother and the strife that she had been giving him. Then another father responded. Then another, and another, and you get the idea. That session moved from the planned interviewing and job skill activities to a discussion on how to improve relationships with their babies' mothers.

It is important to let them know they can share anything with the group at any time. This will also help them realize that you care about how they feel and what they think.

Many of your fathers will experience transportation difficulties. That is understandable at their age, so provide transportation to and from the support groups. If you do not, you may be sitting alone with your chips and Kool-Aid. If you can't offer transportation, give the guys bus passes. Do everything in your power to get them to the meetings. If you have participants with vehicles, ask if they can pick up some of the guys. If they agree, give them an extra incentive for helping you out. A CD or $5 would be cool with most teenagers.

Important advice about offering transportation concerns your choice of music. If you are a Willie Nelson fan, and your teenage dad likes Mobb Deep or DMX, don't force him to listen to your music. Let him listen to what he likes. It will only be playing in your car for ten or fifteen minutes. Your choice of music may not make him leave the program, but it may force him to find alternative transportation. Your acceptance of his music is a symbol of your acceptance of him.

Celebrating Graduation

You have worked hard at recruiting, keeping them in the program, facilitating, providing services, collaborating, and keeping immaculate documentation on your fathers. So what's next? Well, now it's time to celebrate. You deserve it and your fathers deserve it. Reward them for their hard work and progress.

The ROAD program likes to hold a graduation ceremony, somewhat like high school or college, except no caps and gowns. The ROAD program pays for the evening for all the participants and their families.

Find a nice place to have dinner, not a fast-food place. Choose a restaurant where the fathers can sit down to order, a family restaurant or something centered around the children. If there is a private room available for your celebration, reserve it. Chuck E. Cheese is a good place because it's less formal and the dads have a great time. Don't forget to ask the participants what they would like to eat.

Invite the young fathers and their families. The ROAD program generally invites a guest speaker to address the fathers. After all, they have heard us talk long enough. Give out certificates of completion. A small gift adds a nice touch. It doesn't have to be elaborate; maybe a small book or gift certificate.

Invite the local media. The news is often guilty of printing or showing negative images of fathers and teenagers in general. This will be a good time to show off your good guys. It will also give your program some positive and probably much needed attention. The more the community knows about you, the easier it will be to collaborate and receive grant money. Plus, it will give the fathers in your group an extra boost of self-esteem because they are being recognized for something positive. Also very important, positive media attention will help you recruit future clients.

18

Promoting Your Program

Promoting your program is important on several levels. First of all, promotion is the key to finding your participants. The majority will probably come from referring agencies and collaborating partners. However, word of mouth is still the most effective way of getting the word out about your program and the benefits for your participants.

You want to present your program in the most positive light through services you provide, but you also have to learn to be a great promoter. You can't help the young fathers who don't know about your program.

Brochures — How, Where

Websites and brochures are good ways to promote. Budgets can limit your efforts because companies that design brochures can be costly. Find organizations that will provide this service at a reduced or discounted rate, or perhaps someone on your staff can design your brochures and find a printer who will give you a reduced rate. For years, I designed the ROAD program brochures. We printed them ten at a time on the computer and printer in our office. We used heavy stock paper and it was a decent brochure. However, it looked cheap.

Future collaborators and other people may not take your program seriously if your materials aren't perceived as professional. We couldn't do anything about those perceptions because we couldn't produce, financially, the professional looking brochures. Later we received a small grant to print quality brochures. I designed the brochures once again and saved a little money. Trial, error, and patience helped me learn desktop publishing skills. I also designed our website through the same trial and error I experienced with the brochure. Professional designers could do a better job, but doing it ourselves saves money.

The ROAD program also has posters and fliers. Put posters in places teenagers frequent. Get permission to hang posters at local high schools and community colleges. Health centers and doctors' offices are also good locations for your poster.

You could develop a big poster with a stapled-on pocket to hold your brochures plus a little pocket for your business cards.

Make sure the posters are bright enough to catch their eye. The ROAD program uses purple, black, and gray. The purple stands out and almost screams, "LOOK AT ME!"

Fliers and brochures should be given to the fathers in the initial letter you send them. Fliers and brochures should also be given to youth workers and organizations. (If you'd like a copy of the ROAD brochure, please contact us.)

Offer a story about your program to the school newspapers. Most high schools include a few (perhaps many) teen fathers.

Be sure the ministers, social workers, and counselors in your area have brochures and posters. Offer them to employment and welfare offices. You could ask the ministers to include a notice about your young fathers program in their parish newsletter.

What about a classified ad in your local newspaper, perhaps in the Help Wanted section?

Radio, TV Promotion

Public service announcements (PSAs) are another effective way to promote your program. Radio and TV stations often run

PSAs for non-profit organizations. In Roanoke, a local funeral home provides funding for non-profits to promote their program through PSAs. If your locality has businesses that offer these services, contact them immediately and establish a relationship.

The NAACP has a weekly call-in radio show in Roanoke, and they invited me to talk about the importance of fatherhood. I told the listeners about the program and answered questions from callers. Not only did we get the word out about the program, but we also received four referrals immediately. The NAACP also pledged to support us. They promote our program, and they also provided money for one of our ROAD graduations.

Consider Sporting Events

If you live in an area that has minor league or professional sporting events, contact them and ask for free tickets for a father-child or family outing. Minor league baseball games are a great place to begin making contacts. Contact the general manager and ask if you could collaborate on a "Father's Night Out" evening. Ask the team to provide discounted or free tickets for every child that attends the game with his or her dad.

The game could be an event to raise money. If you can persuade them to hold a fundraiser, that would be great. You'd make some much needed money for your program and you would raise the awareness of your mission. Either way, your program will have the opportunity to be recognized which is what you want.

Thinking Outside the Box

The bottom line in promoting is to "think outside the box." You already have a unique perspective in that you work with young fathers. Every non-profit needs to promote their program, so the competition is intense.

Don't be apologetic of the fact that you work mostly with young men. Many people have tried to make us feel bad because we don't focus on women in our services. Don't argue with them, but accentuate the positive effects of your program. Children are the number one reason we do what we do, and all children need their fathers.

Young fathers are often pushed away. Instead, you are ensuring that your clients are a positive influence in their children's lives, not only financially, but also emotionally. No matter how you choose to market your program, be positive and be certain of your goals.

Advocating for Young Fathers

It is important as an educator, and one that is knowledgeable on the subject of fatherhood, to advocate for *all* fathers, not just the ones in your program. Become involved in community meetings regarding teen pregnancy or adolescent issues. Too many tend to berate teenagers, especially teenage fathers. You must be the one to stand up for them.

A good place to start is with the media. Whenever you are doing something special, call the local newspaper and television stations and let them know about it. Write articles or letters to the editor concerning young fathers, especially if something negative is written or printed about them. It is not only your job, but also your moral duty to promote responsible fatherhood.

You may contact the National Fatherhood Initiative, The Virginia Fatherhood Campaign, or the ROAD program to receive tips and advice on how to be an effective advocate for your program and fathers everywhere. The National Center for Strategic Nonprofit Planning and Community Leadership also has wonderful professionals who are master advocates for fragile families.

19

Working with Incarcerated Fathers

Many of the programs for incarcerated fathers have developed from already existing programs that work with ex-offenders and within the prison system. Providing a component for incarcerated fathers is challenging, but can be an extremely rewarding experience for your program and for the fathers who participate.

Correlli Rasheed is currently the fatherhood case manager for the Fatherhood and Families Program at Total Action Against Poverty (TAP) in Roanoke, VA. Before coming to Fatherhood and Families, he was the institutional liaison for TAP VA CARES (Virginia Community Action Re-entry System) and has over twenty years experience working with incarcerated fathers and their families. Rasheed sees many benefits in working with incarcerated fathers.

"The reality is that these fathers we serve in the prisons will one day get out, and their children will be a tremendous influence on whether they choose to live the kind of lifestyle that will not put them back in prison," says Rasheed. The program helps participants understand the impact they will have on their children's lives. Their involvement will be better for their children, and will also reduce recidivism for the fathers.

Most Grew Up Without a Dad

Most incarcerated men grew up in a home without a father. In fact, over seventy percent of incarcerated juveniles grew up in a home without a dad, according to Wade Horn, *Father Facts* (2002: National Fatherhood Initiative [NFI]). Your program could be a great influence in ending that cycle. The NFI has developed a curriculum titled *Long Distance Dads* by Randell D. Turner and Martha C. Eichenlaub (1998). One of the main points of the curriculum is to address and stop the cycle of incarcerated men who have grown up in a home without a father.

"The responsibility involved in fatherhood is similar to the responsibility all men need to have to live a productive lifestyle," says Rasheed. For any person to change their destructive lifestyle or habits, they have to want to. Part of this necessary change may begin with their children. Providing a support network for the dads can enable them to understand how their actions affect (negatively and positively) not only themselves, but also the people that depend on them.

Support Group Important Here, Too

The support group is extremely important for incarcerated participants. Just like the support programs you facilitate elsewhere, incarcerated fathers need a place to vent as well as to become empowered by the other fathers.

"They can express emotions in the group that they can't elsewhere. It also helps alleviate some of the stress they encounter with being incarcerated and having their children away from them," says Rasheed.

The bonding taking place between fathers in a group is powerful. It can also help bring different groups in the prison system together, groups that normally wouldn't talk to each other.

Rasheed explains what makes the groups so effective. "Dads of all ages are included in the support groups. The older fathers often tell of their regrets and talk about their mistakes, and the younger guys can listen to this and apply the situation to their own lives. Some of the older guys are even talking about becoming grandfathers and how they were not there for their own kids, but they hope to be there for their grandchildren."

The support group, says Rasheed, is very similar to the support groups that are facilitated for non-incarcerated fathers. "We discuss responsible decision making, male-female relationships, and values just like we do in other support groups."

One thing that needs to be discussed in the support groups is child support. Child support laws will vary depending on the state you live in so it is imperative you become acquainted with the laws in your locality. For instance, in Virginia, child support orders will not be forgiven because you are incarcerated. The best that can happen for a father who is incarcerated in Virginia is to have his support order reduced to $65 per month. Let the fathers know what the law is and how they can go about filing appeals or motions to reduce the order.

Your state may forgive an incarcerated dad of the child support payments while he is incarcerated. Contact your local child support office to educate yourself on the law and what you must do to help him. Collaborate with child support and ask a representative to accompany you to the prison every two or three months. Be mindful that this could be a tough sell. Child support officials may not want to accompany a fatherhood counselor to a prison setting.

Communicating Through Letters

Other activities that can be done in the prison setting are letter writing campaigns. Rasheed helps the fathers get in touch with their true emotions and helps them learn how to communicate effectively with their children. Incarcerated fathers may tend to write about things such as the weather or how school is going for the children. Fathers, however, need to be more involved than that, and the support group can help them get in touch with their feelings. The goal is not to depress the children or to burden them, but to help the father talk about real issues that are affecting his family.

"Every week, we open the meetings by asking them who had contact with their children. We talk about issues discussed and the difficulty in conveying those feelings to their children," says

Rasheed. The father needs to feel comfortable communicating, and this is a learned skill. Many incarcerated men in prison will tell you that communication was not an everyday occurrence in their home.

Another way for the fathers to communicate with their children is through tapes. You could tape a father reading a story to his child (only his child isn't beside him), then send the tape to the mother to play for their child.

Rasheed also talked about the disadvantages for the incarcerated fathers. "Fathers come into the group and become emotionally charged up about their children, yet they can't see their kids for another four or five years. When group is over, they must go back to their cells."

Keeping the emotion and the passion of being a good father is difficult in the prison setting. The dads are learning good communication skills, parenting skills, and getting support from other fathers, but they can't apply it in the real world.

Another difficulty is that the fathers, when released, tend to go home to other areas of the state where there may not be a fatherhood program. The support will no longer be there for them. You will want to do all you can to meet dads returning to your city or town. At the time of their release, they can have immediate contact with your program because of your intervention. VA CARES is unique in the fact that the program is run statewide in various localities.

Requirements for In-Prison Work

If you are going to work with incarcerated fathers, there are some guidelines that some institutions require before you can enter. Some prisons will not allow ex-offenders to come back into the prison to facilitate these meetings. This makes no sense at all to me. Fathers and men who have lived that life know better than anyone else what it takes to turn one's life around. Ex-offenders can get their point across better, in most situations, than those who have a clean record.

You will have to go through an extensive background check before you are allowed in the prison. You will be fingerprinted as well. If your program employs ex-offenders, be aware that they may not be allowed to run your prison outreach. However, even with all the restrictions and regulations you must meet, it is well worth your time and effort to work with incarcerated fathers. Even if your participant returns to a city that doesn't have a fatherhood program, he will be helped by your involvement.

Developing Program for Incarcerated Dads

Robert Pacheco directed the Teen Parenting Skills Project at the Bernalillo County Juvenile Detention Center, Albuquerque, NM, 1993-2001. Pacheco reports that the program began as a request from line staff at the facility to address the needs of an 18-year-old father of two sons, and developed into an eight-year program. Until this time, Detention Center policy allowed for only parents, grandparents, or a spouse to visit.

First, Pacheco asked the director for guidance on what the facility could offer this young man. The director would allow visitation privileges under several terms: parenting classes be provided, facility staff be asked for input concerning the restrictions they would like to see, and that visitation hours be outside the normal visitation schedule of the facility.

Pacheco soon found a teacher in the Albuquerque Public Schools system, Ms. Dale Bolson, willing to teach a parenting class.

The next step was to ask line staff what issues would need to be addressed in setting up a parenting skills program with visitation privileges attached to it. Those concerns included contraband being brought in by visitors and rule violations by the teen father. How would they deal with these situations? Strip searches of teens are required after any family visitation.

"So, Dale and I began to gather information that would address classes aimed at teenage parents," Pacheco explained. "We asked the New Mexico Teen Pregnancy Coalition for assistance. We attended a resource committee meeting and shared our project with those in attendance. We quickly learned that there were programs for teen mothers, but none for teen fathers. Also, there were *no* programs addressing the juveniles incarcerated in our state facilities.

"We were directed to the Peanut Butter and Jelly Program in Albuquerque, NM, in particular the IMPACT Program that works with incarcerated adults in the prison system. It was here that we learned a great deal about topics important to provide to inmates."

Participation Is Voluntary

By the time the first class was held, a second teen father had volunteered. This young man had heard that this program was going to allow him visits with his sons. As the news of the program spread throughout the facility, several teenage mothers were referred. The program was offered to any teenage parents, pregnant or parenting, incarcerated in the building. The primary focus was on teenage fathers, as the population in the facility is 90 percent males, but the first co-ed classes soon began.

Classes lasting 90 minutes were scheduled weekly plus visits on Saturday morning for one hour. The program was set up to take teen parents on a voluntary basis.

Classes were held after the regular school program was completed for the day. Having visitation on Saturday avoided regular visitation days. The teen parents were advised that if they were placed on room restrictions for violating facility rules, and were not able to participate in the program on the day of class, they would lose the opportunity to have a visit for that week.

Several issues helped start the program and continue it for several years: program facilitators conducted classes on their own time, after regular scheduled hours; there were no requests for funding from the facility; visitation was supervised by the program facilitators, so no requests were made to use facility staffing.

The program began with donated books from several sources. Their first funding was through a local used car lot owner who gave $300 to buy books. They also applied for grants through the Albuquerque Public Schools Join-A-School program, and received two $500 grants to buy educational materials.

"As the program developed we were able to seek out community agencies working with teenage mothers and ask that they adapt some of their programming to reach the males," Pacheco commented. "As we attended workshops on adolescent pregnancy, we let people know how the population of teenage parents at the Detention Center needed services."

Pacheco and Bolson asked community programs to consider coming into the Detention Center to present information on parenting, share information on their programs, and advise the teens on services available to them when they would be released.

"Particularly important in working with incarcerated teenage parents is to help them understand that even though you are incarcerated, you never stop being a parent. The need to continue some form of communication with their partner and child is extremely important. It is a constant topic of discussion with this group.

"Phone contact is limited in the facility," Pacheco continued, "and when contact is made with the partner, the conversation needs to be pleasant and not controlling. The teen fathers often feel the need to control the female while they are incarcerated. They do this by checking up through family and friends on the partner's comings and goings, then confronting the partner over the phone. Obviously, the female hangs the phone up and does not show up for the visit!"

Helping participants improve their communication skills with their partner is a very crucial part of the program. Also, teaching letter writing skills is important. Letters to their partner and child show they are thinking about their families while in detention, especially important if that partner and child is out of town or has limited access to transportation.

In 2000, the Juvenile Detention Center was chosen as one of the first five sites to demonstrate the New Mexico Young Fathers Project funded by the New Mexico Department of Health. The project is working with the teenage fathers who participate in the teen parenting project in the facility. Case management services are provided through weekly group plus one-on-one counseling. The emphasis is on assisting the young father in establishing a positive plan to follow when he is released. Employment, educational opportunities, and group programs in the community are among the services they provide. A big piece of the puzzle missing from the Detention Center program was follow-up after release. The Young Fathers Project is a great asset to the teen fathers.

Pacheco's Suggestions

Pacheco suggests that anyone wishing to begin a teen-parenting program in a detention type facility follow these steps:

1. Approach the director of the facility and get his/her blessing.

2. Find someone in the facility that champions your cause – they can help you get through all the security issues. They can also help recruit other staff support.

3. Secure funding that will allow the purchase of educational materials that can be given to the teens. This allows them to share with their partners at visitation.

4. Recruit community agency support. Assure them they will be safe if they present programming in a detention center. Remind them that many of these teens need their services.

5. Media coverage of your services as "a unique program offered to juveniles" could be a positive sell to the facility.

6. Be ready to volunteer your time to community agencies in trade for them presenting programs in the facility. Volunteer for a board of directors position. This would allow you to bring up your cause at every opportunity.

Whenever possible, encourage the teen fathers to be the best dads they can be. Remind them not to be afraid of making mistakes in providing care to their child. They need to try not to worry about what their partners say or the looks they receive when interacting with their child. For their child's sake, they need to be respectful to the mother of their child, even if they are not living together.

20

Putting Out the Green Beans

The Fatherhood and Families team was recently at our weekly Monday morning staff meeting. During the meeting, we talk about program objectives, paperwork, legislative issues, employment issues, etc., but we also have time set aside to discuss the fathers with whom we are working. We do this to keep everyone up to date on all the dads because we want to be as personable as possible. That is often hard when a staff of six is working with more than 100 dads and their families per year. This time also gives the staff an opportunity to discuss the best way to approach a specific client.

This particular staff meeting started out like so many others, but when it came time for the staff to share the events of their week, we were given a metaphor for the whole program.

A young dad, age 22, had been working at a local cafeteria for about two months. He had a child support payment of $150 per month and arrearages of about $1,500. His prior work history was not stellar to say the least. He had a high school diploma and had never held a full-time job longer than six months.

He arrived at work one morning and found the new district manager was there for the day. District managers often have a way of throwing their weight around like no other employee of a company. This particular district manager was new, and he was determined to establish himself as the man in charge. After all, he couldn't let anyone feel he didn't know what he was doing.

Our young father was setting up the food for the hot bar as he had done every day for the past two months. His job was to bring the food from the kitchen to the food line, make sure the food line was kept neat, inform the kitchen when a particular item was running low, and replace that item. He loved his job because he was able to talk to many of the people that came through the line for lunch or dinner.

As he was putting out the mashed potatoes, the district manager walked up behind him and asked, "Where are the green beans?"

"I'm going to get them in a minute," our young father replied.

"Get them now, the lunch rush is coming any minute," ordered the manager.

Our young father retreated to the kitchen and brought out the pan of creamed corn. The district manager walked quickly back to our young father and said, "I thought I told you to bring out the green beans?"

"I'll get them in a minute," said our father.

"You'll get them right now."

Our young dad was getting upset. "I said I'll get them in a minute, I only have two hands, and you ain't got to talk to me like I'm a dog, I'm a man."

At this time the other employees were watching the exchange between the new district manager and the employee.

"Come to the office. We need to discuss this in private," said the manager.

As our young father walked into the office, the district manager began to yell. "You do not defy me or show me disrespect out there. I told you to put out the green beans, and I meant put out the green beans."

"First of all, I'm doing my job, and you start ordering me around like I'm a dog or something. I'm a man and you better treat me like a man or next time I'm gonna smack you."

"What did you say?"

"I said I'm gonna smack you if you don't treat me with some respect," replied our father.

"You're fired. Get out and don't come back," said the manager.

The young father told this story at the support group meeting and was trying to defend himself and justify his actions. "He can't talk to me like that. Not for no $6.75 an hour."

The fatherhood counselors tried to explain that the job could be a stepping-stone, and he needed the job for future references. The young father was adamant in his position, and all the persuasion of the fatherhood counselors did nothing to change his mind.

Finally, tired of the stalemate between the father and the counselors, one of the other participants threw up his hands and said, "Man, just put out the green beans."

Everyone stopped and looked at the bold participant.

"If you would have just put out the damn green beans you'd still have a job. Now you're unemployed like us. How are you going to tell your kids you got fired over some stupid green beans?"

Everyone started laughing in agreement with the other father.

So, "Just put out the green beans" is our new program metaphor. It is a metaphor for life as well. We are always going to have pushy bosses who breathe down our neck. We are always going to have things that we don't want to do. But if we "just put out the green beans," we will prevail and win out in the end. This doesn't mean we must let people disrespect us or our fathers, but often times the battles we fight are of little matter and could be resolved if we would "just put out the green beans."

Needless to say, when anyone in our office starts complaining about things that happen in our life or with our bosses, there is always someone there to tell us to "put out the green beans."

Don't ever let "green beans" come between you and your client. Do what you need to do to help young fathers become caring, involved, and financially supportive parents. You *will* make a difference.

Everybody wins when Dad's involved.

The roads to fatherhood taken by the young men depicted in this book were clearly affected by their personal fatherhood experiences and their personal choices. The insights Jon Morris shares from his experience working with young men clearly demonstrate how complicated and challenging it is to address the fear, anger or frustration young men have when they face fatherhood too early. It is obvious that there is much these young men need to learn in order to become positively engaged fathers, contributors to their own community, and personally fulfilled. Who will be there for them so that they can be there for their children? People like Jon Morris.

The question we should ask is what other individuals, committed professionals, and organizations can do to take these stories and create solutions for the young men that are not yet ready to be fathers. Isaiah, Curtis and Jacob are vivid examples of young men that reside in our communities. They have exposed their young lives to us and serve as teachers of real life feelings, experiences, and consequences, but we must understand that the ending to their stories remains unwritten. Whether we can interpret solutions or strategies that work in our own communities will depend on whether we feel the topic of fatherhood is sufficiently worthwhile to pursue. However, if we focus on what is right for the children of these young men, perhaps our efforts will have a clearer purpose and be more easily undertaken.

We understand that young men who have children too early require immediate support in order to avoid the pitfall of paternal disengagement and inability to be self-sustaining. But other supports should exist *before* they have their first child. Does anyone bother to stop and ask young men whether they understand the reality of what it takes to raise happy and healthy children? Did they ever *want* to have children? How many children do they want to nurture and guide? Who did they envision their partner to be? Their answers should affect the approach we take and how we share information with them.

If this seems too much for one person, rest assured that there is plenty of work for all of us. Our valuable front line staff should be afforded training to build skills to work effectively with young men and fathers. Coordinators and directors of prevention or intervention programs have to consider that some young men do not walk through our doors because they know we are not ready to receive them. And executive directors and boards of directors must understand that building effective programs to engage young men requires resources to match the need and willingness to do business in new ways.

Too often the programs we initiate flounder when organizational support is not present. We then look to staff to determine why our efforts are disappointing without considering the potential for failure organizations create because of this lack of support.

But the topics addressed in *Road to Fatherhood* also ask us to consider what communities can do to help young men develop into healthy, happy, and wholesome young people. Jon Morris' approach is not a one size fits all. Rather, he integrates services and information while balancing the appropriate dosage of support to meet the needs of each young man served. Some things that he does are easy for all members of a community to understand and support such as:

- Helping young men understand their own familial values and how they will adopt or adapt those values in their personal lives;
- Recognizing that they are valued and supported for their potential as they cultivate their positive purpose in life;
- Informing our schools that all young men should receive an education that allows them to develop their career or vocational interest;
- Reinforcing the idea that we expect young men to grow up to be responsible productive citizens; and
- Providing young men with the benefit of seeing both men and women as positive role models within their community so that they can see themselves in the same manner.

However, there are other equally important topics that young men need to talk about as they grow up and mature. And for some of these we encounter trepidation and concern. Among these topics are:

- Extending medical services to young men to match their age, development and life experience;
- Developing programs that allow young men safety to explore who they want to be without judgment;
- Valuing young people enough to create youth-adult partnerships when developing new programs intended for their benefit;
- Determining whether a young man gets more attention if he is a juvenile offender than when he obtains educational success;
- Opening discussions about issues such as fatherhood, sexual development, and reproductive health; and
- Offering a young man and/or his family needed services and allowing them to leave our agencies with their dignity fully intact.

Our challenge is mustering the resolve to do that which is overwhelmingly supported *and* that which we know is right for young men, their family, and the community.

Native American elders teach that we are caretakers of what
we have and our decisions will affect the next seven generations.
When we overlook the young men that are struggling to make
life choices that are in their own best interest, especially those
who already have children, then what is in store for us in the next
generation? If Jon Morris' ideas lead us to create and develop
effective programs for young men, what will be the outcome?

Because change occurs slowly, I suspect that, like the elders
of seven generations past, we will not reap the full benefits of
our efforts. However, the parents, life partners, and children of
future young men will. Perhaps we may come to understand that
young men have a positive role to play in the success of their
family. They may see that the safety and development of their
community depends on whether they can be unselfish stewards.
They will continue to be, just as they are now, reflections of
all of us.

And what would be the outcome if we move ahead with a
good heart, sincere intentions, and informed decisions? That is a
question we each must answer both alone and collectively.
Hopefully, the direction of the road we construct in our
communities can be one that eventually leads us to the road that
Jon is helping to construct for his.

With deep respect for my parents, teachers and elders,

                                                    Héctor Sánchez-Flores

*Héctor is a Senior Research Associate at the Center for
Reproductive Health Research and Policy at the University of
California, San Francisco, and is thankful to the staff and
participants of California's Male Involvement Programs. He
lives in Santa Clara, California, with his wife, Lucila.*

Appendix

She needs her daddy's love and emotional as well as financial support.

Outreach/Recruitment Strategies

1. Go through the young mothers to find the fathers of their children. Visit
   a) family planning or prenatal clinics
   b) hospital maternity wards
   c) teen pregnancy and teen mom programs
   d) well baby clinics
   e) welfare-to-work programs.

2. Commit adequate resources and staff time for outreach activities. Help administrators and funders recognize that recruitment and retention take time.

3. Seek referrals from
   a) child support enforcement agencies
   b) social service agencies
   c) juvenile justice system
   d) school counselors.
   Establish personal relationships with specific staff who will get to know and respect your program and who will be highly motivated to make referrals.

4. Recruit staff who can relate to young fathers and gain their trust. Involve experienced participants or program graduates as paid or volunteer peer leaders and outreach workers.

5. Involve program participants in recruitment. Offer awards or dollars for successful recruitment. Have staff and participants make presentations to other program providers, schools, child support staff, etc. Feature participants in TV/public service announcements.

6. Make it easier for fathers to attend by providing bus fare and/ or other forms of transportation.

7. As much as possible, maintain an "open door" policy. Be ready when fathers are. Be prepared to give those who drop out another chance.

8. Have flexible schedules to accommodate fathers' life situations, particularly as they become successfully involved in education, training, and employment.

9. Use posters and fliers, but remember that word-of-mouth contacts are usually most effective.

10. Use media messages — PSAs on radio and TV, interviews in newspaper articles, etc. Advertise on radio stations that the fathers listen to. Don't forget the Internet. A lot of young men do "surf."

11. Develop a catchy slogan or program name (e.g. ROAD – Reaching Out to Adolescent Dads).

12. Do street outreach. Develop a very short "blurb" to deliver to potential participants on the street. Knock on doors. Be patient, persistent, and respectful. Outwait them.

13. In brochures or posters, be sure to use language that is reading-level appropriate.

14. Avoid screening procedures that weed out the young men who are most in need of services.

15. Other outreach techniques include:
    a. setting up a table at community events, fairs, etc.
    b. conducting community surveys and informing people about your program.
    c. establishing programs in prisons and setting up a follow-up for fathers when they are released.
    d. recruiting at multiple points of contact — schools, recreation centers, churches, job placement programs, malls, basketball courts, street corners, etc.

Developed by NPCL, Washington, DC, 2001
www.NPCL.org
Reprinted with permission

Retention Strategies

1. Staff must be effective and caring, recognizing that these young men have been let down by many adults in their lives. Often they test staff to determine if they are "for real" or if they are doing this work for their own egos. It's important for staff to pass the test and to come across as approachable and nonjudgmental. Staff must also be strong role models who display the attributes that the young men are trying to acquire. Young fathers often get hooked because there is a staff person around who will be there for them.

2. Find ways to engage fathers in the program early on — perhaps by matching them up with current participants.

3. Encourage a sense of ownership in the program. In peer support groups, have participants guide your choices of topics and activities.

4. Encourage a positive sense of membership in the program, perhaps with membership cards, T-shirts, or buttons. Have group members decide what symbols they'd like to connote group membership.

5. Provide a nurturing atmosphere — provide snacks; have interesting posters on the wall; have pictures of fathers and children on the walls. Even if you operate in shared space, try to create an identity for your space, particularly areas where fathers gather.

6. Help manage some of the crises that keep fathers from attending. Have funds available for emergency situations.

7. Seek feedback on a regular basis.

8. Offer activities for families where fathers can bring their children on weekends. Build in some purely recreational activities.

9. Call participants who have been absent to find out what's going on. When people who've been absent return, tell them they were missed.

Developed by NPCL, Washington, DC, 1997 <www.NPCL.org>

Reaching Out to Adolescent Dads

Meeting Dates and Topics
for Support Group

All Groups Start Promptly at 6:00 PM

June 14	Introduction and Responsibility
June 28	Contraception and STIs
July 12	**Employment**
July 26	Decision Making
August 9	Manhood/Fatherhood Today
August 23	**CHILD SUPPORT**
September 6	A Daddy's Influence
September 20	Seven Secrets
October 4	**Jimmy Robinson, Attorney**
October 18	Conflict Resolution
November 1	Helping Your Child Learn
November 15	10 Years Later????
November 29	Putting It All Together
December 13	**GRADUATION**

Reaching Out to Adolescent Dads, TAP, 145 Campbell Avenue SW, Roanoke, VA 24011
540.345.6781, ext. 4430; fax 540.777.0225

Fatherhood & Families
Referral Form

Please complete as much of the sheet as you can and mail the referral form to
TAP, Fatherhood & Families, PO Box 2868, Roanoke, VA 24001.

Participant Information

Name _____ Date of Birth _____

Address _____ Zip Code _____

Phone Number _____ School (if applicable) _____

Your Organization's Information

Organization _____ Phone _____

Contact Person _____

Comments or special considerations: _____

_____

Court referred person must ENROLL in 14 business days

Court Use Only

Is the referred person court-ordered or is this a condition of
probation? ___ Court Case Number _____ SSN ___

Review Date _____ COMPLIANT OR NON-COMPLIANT

Signature of referred person _____ **Date** ____

TAP Use Only

Participant Eligible for _____

Children _____

Mother of Children _____ Custody Situation ____

Work _____ Intake _____

Child Support Information _____

Fatherhood & Families
TAP 141 Campbell Ave. SW Roanoke, VA 24011
540.345.6781 x 4430   Fax 540.777.0225
Fathers at Work   For Males Only   Reaching Out to Adolescent Dads
White Copy-Fathers at Work   Yellow Copy-File copy
Pink Copy-Referring Agency   Goldenrod Copy-Client Copy

Road Intake Survey

Name_____ Report Date_____

Case #_____ Start Date _____

Staff Name _____

Age	Ethnic Group	Education	Referred By	
13-15	Native American	0-3 years	Resource	
16-17	Asian	4-6 years	Mothers	
18-19	Black	7-10 years	RAHP	
20-21	Hispanic	11-12 years	CHIP	
22-25	White	13+ years	23-A	
25+	Other	GED	PPBR	

Work	Occupation	Income	Family Member	
Not looking	Skilled Labor	Welfare benefits	Friend	
Full-time	Professional	Less than $5,000	DSS	
Part-time	Fast-food	$5,000-$10,000	Newspaper	
Unemployed	Managerial	$10,000-$15,000	Group Home	
Disabled	Technical	$15,000-$20,000	Schools	
Other	Other	$20,000+	RCHD	
			Other	

Marital Status: Single ___ Married___ Divorced___

Paternity Established   Yes___ No___ Legal Custody Status_____

Amount of Informal Support_____

Child Support Order? Yes___   No___ Amount? _____

Average support payments?_____

Severity Index

Characteristic	Period	Characteristic	Period
Learning Disability		Poor Health	
Received Welfare Benefits		Previous Incarceration	
Father Absent		Family drug abuse	

Comments:

ROAD Tracking Sheet

Date													
1													
2													
3													
4													
5													
6													
7													
8													
9													
10													
Total Present													

Reaching Out to Adolescent Dads, TAP, 145 Campbell Avenue SW, Roanoke, VA 24011. 540.345.6781, ext. 4430; fax 540.777.0225

ROAD Participant Plan

Name _____   Date _____   Staff _____

Rank	Objective	Methods	Measure	Persons Responsible	Estimate/ Actual Time	Achieved (Yes/No)
1	Fathers won't cause more pregnancies.	Family Life education	No repeat fatherhood while enrolled in program.			
2	Teen fathers will establish paternity.	Petition Court	Have teen fathers file necessary paperwork to legally establish paternity.			
3	Teen fathers will pay child support.	Have court order or receipts of payments.	Child support is paid 6 consecutive months w/o failure.			
4	Teen fathers will obtain & sustain legal employment.	Job search, interviewing methods, outreach, and referrals.	Teen father will work, full or part-time, depending on school.			
5	Teen fathers will be involved in raising their child.	Home visits, super- vised visitation, group support.	Increased frequency of child visits, and more communication w/mother.			

ROAD Participant Plan — Additional Objectives

Rank	Objective	Methods	Measure	Persons Responsible	Estimate/Actual Time	Achieved (Yes/No)
6						
7						
8						
9						

Signatures:
Participant _____ Case Manager _____ Completion Date _____

Reaching Out to Adolescent Dads

Weekly Update Sheet

1. Have you seen your child this week? If yes, how often?

2. What activities did you do with your child?

3. Did you pay child support this week? If yes, how much? If no, why not?

4. Have you talked with your baby's mother this week? If yes, how was the conversation?

5. Did you buy Pampers, formula, clothes, etc., during the past week?

6. Are you employed this week?
   Same job___ New job___ No job___
   Just hired at_____

7. Have you missed any school or work this week? If yes, why?

Reaching Out to Adolescent Dads, TAP, 145 Campbell Avenue SW, Roanoke, VA 24011
540.345.6781, ext. 4430; fax 540.777.0225

ROAD Father Assessment
Part 1

Name _____ Date of Birth _____

Address _____

Phone #_____ Social Security # _____

Partner/Spouse/Child's Mother _____

Children and Ages _____

Interview Date _____ Interviewer _____

Category Indicator	Intake	Follow Up	Exit
Education			
Working toward GED			
Currently in high school			
Non-high school completer			
GED attainment			
H.S. diploma			
Trade or technical school diploma			
College degree			
Employment			
Unemployed			
Part-time temporary			
Part-time permanent			
Full-time temporary			
Full-time permanent			
Disability			
Housing			
Public Housing			
Shelter			
Permanent Housing			
Lives with baby's mother			
Owns Home			
Renting			
Other			

Category Indicator	Intake	Follow Up	Exit
Health/Lifestyle			
Unprotected sex			
Multiple Partners			
Relationship only with child's mother			
Protected sex			
Income			
No means of support			
Welfare			
Dependent			
Independent			
Drugs/Alcohol			
Uncontrolled use			
Periodic and problematic			
Enrolled in treatment program			
Non-user			
Recreational			
Transportation			
No means of transportation			
Public transit			
Depend on others			
Own transportation			
Relationship with Law			
Currently incarcerated			
On probation			
Previous probate/incarcerated			
No problem			
Relationship with child			
Unattached legally and emotionally			
Legally attached, emotionally unattached			
Legally unattached, emotionally attached			
Child support payments only			
Legally attached – emotionally attached			
Association with child			
Visits once a year or less			
Visits once every six months			
Visits monthly			
Visits weekly			
Daily involvement			
Lives with child			

Comments

ROAD Father Assessment
Part 2

Name _____ Date of Birth _____

Address _____

Phone # _____ Social Security # _____

Child's Mother _____

Interview Date _____ Interviewer _____

Children	M/F	Age	School/ Grade	Lives with	How long?

Involvement	Daily	1-2 wk	3-4 wk	1-2 mo	3-4 mo	Hardly ever
How often do you see your child?						
Do you help with homework?						
Do you participate in child's activities?						
When you are with your child, how often do you watch TV?						
Cook or prepare food together?						
Talk to your child?						
Help with dressing or hygiene?						
Play with your child?						
How much time would you like to spend with your child?						

Children's Activities	N/A	Not much	Average	A lot
Does your child enjoy books?				
Is your child involved in organized sports?				
How well does your child get along with other kids?				
Does your child seem to respect your authority?				
Does your child appear to be happy?				
How well do you like being a dad?				

ROAD Father Assessment
Part 2 - Cont.

Children's Activities	N/A	Not much	Average	A lot

*Reaching Out to Adolescent Dads, TAP, 145 Campbell Avenue SW, Roanoke, VA 24011
540.345.6781, ext. 4430; fax 540.777.0225*

ROAD Outcome Evaluation

Outcome	Measure	Data Interval	Data Source	Target
1 Teen fathers will not contribute to repeat pregnancies.	No repeat fatherhood while enrolled in program.	Monthly.	Self report.	75%
2 Teen fathers will establish paternity.	The number or % of teen fathers whose name is on the child's birth certificate.	Monthly or as paternity is legally established.	Self report. Report from mother. Copy court document.	75%
3 Maximize the % of dads who pay their child support regularly.	Child support is paid monthly w/o exception for 6 months.	Every six months.	Self report. Report from mother.	60%
4 Teen fathers will obtain and sustain legal employment.	Teen father will get a full-time or part-time job, depending on school status.	Monthly and at graduation.	Employment records. Self report. Employer.	70%
5 Teen fathers will be involved in raising their child.	Increased frequency of visits with child. Increased frequency of communication with mother.	Monthly.	Self report. Report from mother.	70%

Reaching Out to Adolescent Dads, TAP, 145 Campbell Avenue SW, Roanoke, VA 24011
540.345.6781, ext. 4430; fax 540.777.0225

ROAD Participant Review

Client #: _____   Staff: _____
Date: _____

Objective	P/S *	Achieved yes/no	Barriers	Comments
1				
2				
3				
4				
5				
6				
7				
8				

* P/S = Primary/Secondary Goal

Objectives Achieved This Period			
# achieved this period	Percent	# achieved cumulative	Percent

*Reaching Out to Adolescent Dads, TAP, 145 Campbell Avenue SW, Roanoke, VA 24011
540.345.6781, ext. 4430; fax 540.777.0225*

ROAD Response Form

_____Date

1. What did you like most about the ROAD program?

2. What did you like least about it?

3. If you could make changes to the program, what would you do?

4. Please answer on a scale of 1 to 10 (10 being the highest)

Staff is accessible. ____

I feel the staff cares about me. ____

Staff is knowledgeable about their job. ____

Support groups are educational and fun. ____

Staff keeps their word. ____

Staff makes me feel welcome. ____

Staff gets my input. ____

5. Would you recommend another father join the program?

6. Additional comments:

Sources of Information on Fatherhood Programs

The National Fatherhood
  Initiative
One Bank Street, Suite 160
Gaithersburg, MD 20878
301.948.0599
301.948.4325 (fax)
www.fatherhood.org

The Virginia Fatherhood
  Campaign
Virginia Department of Health
1500 E. Main Street, Room 105
Richmond, VA 23219
804.692.0400
www.vdh.state.va.us
Once on the web page, click on
"Select an office," then *"Family
health services,"* and then
"Involvement of fathers."

Partners for Fragile Families
National Center for Strategic
  Nonprofit Planning and
  Community Leadership (NPCL)
1155 Connecticut Avenue, NW
Washington, DC 20036
202.429.6526
www.npcl.org

National Center of Fathers and
  Families
Philadelphia Children's Network
P.O. Box 5919
1650 Arch Street, 16th Floor
Philadelphia, PA 19102-9119
(215) 686-3910

The Father Development Project
108 Whitewood Road, Suite 4
Charlottesville, VA 22901
434.978.1773
434.978.4049 (fax)
www.fatherdevelopment.net

Reaching Out to Adolescent Dads
  (ROAD)
Total Action Against Poverty
145 Campbell Avenue SW
Roanoke, VA 24011
540.345.6781 x 4430
540.777.0225 (fax)
www.roadprogram.org

Words From Our Fathers

I wanted to have a space so the fathers could express the kind of dads they want to be. The following contains letters that the participants wrote during a support group. The activity was for each father to pretend his child was 20 years old. He was to imagine what he would want his child to say about him. The letters were very powerful. We used the letters as a springboard as to what future goals they would have to reach for their letters to come true. I think you will find the letters as touching as I did. These letters also show that not all young fathers want to be absent in their children's lives.

My father is a serious man who only wants the best because it is his way of thinking. He told me that when I was young, he was going to be successful. He made it up in his mind that he wasn't going to settle for anything less than the best for me. He is a hard worker who is dedicated to me first and that makes me proud, and second he encourages me to do the right things in life because he knows life is a struggle and life will make or break you. My father, even though he is not with my mother, is very respectful to my mother and always talks to her about my grades, life, and me. Though my father has his own business, he makes sure that I am taken care of and I really appreciate all the time and attention he gives me. He's always on the move but he makes sure I'm OK. I care for my dad and want to follow in his footsteps, his hard work, dedication, respect, and his success.

Michael, age 17 — Son, Elijah, 2 years old

There are many things I can say about my dad, but I'll only mention a few. Some things I really didn't come to understand as a child, that I did later learn about him. Now that I have a very good relationship with him, I believe I have the best father and son relationship in the world.

In the early years of my life, I had a lot of ill resentment towards my dad because he was never there. My mom told me so many bad things about him, that later I came to believe it, because he never was around at all. And later when he did try and contact me, because of my hardness, I had no desire to be with him.

Later as I began to see how earnest and determined he was to be with me, I saw that he was being sincere about actually being my dad. It was through this I began to see that all these things about my dad wasn't true, and I wouldn't trade my dad in for the world.

DeCarlos, age 24 — Son, Isaiah, 2 years old

I want my kids to feel like they have the greatest dad in the world because I am the type of dad that is always gonna be there even though I have two kids basically the same age. I can still do the same for both of them. I want them to feel free to come to me whenever with whatever problem they may have. I want to be able to enjoy life with them together, not separated.

David, age 23 — Son, DeJuan, 8 months; daughter, Qwonneshia, 7 months

My daddy is the most honest guy in the world. He tries his best at making things work for me. My daddy is a hard worker and he supports me even though I am 21 years old. He loves everything I do and the way I do them. My dad is the most loving man in the world. I think my dad should get father of the year. My dad is very self protective of me and he won't let anyone hurt me.

Chris, age 15 — Daughter, Nakeisha, 1 year

My Daddy,

The coolest of dads who is down to earth and very loving and caring. I love my dad because he spent quality time with me when I was younger, no matter what. Even if he was tired when he came home from work or whatever, he spent time with me. My father kept it real with me dealing with everything in life, in dealing with sex, drugs, and guys. He always guided me down the right road, he preached and preached to me about doing well in school or whatever it was I was participating in. We never had much but he made sure that we had things such as a place to live, food in our mouths, and clothes on our backs. My daddy was a hard worker and didn't play around when it came to money.

Jermaine, age 20 — Daughters, Kyndra, 1, and Alexis, 2 years old

BIBLIOGRAPHY

Dozens of books about parenting are published each year, a few especially for teenage fathers. The titles listed below include titles for professionals who work with teen parents as well as titles of interest to young dads. Also included is a listing of videos appropriate for showing to teen fathers and their partners.

The address and phone number of a publisher is listed only with the first resource described. Prices quoted are current at press time (2002). Because prices change so rapidly, however, and because publishers move, call your local library reference department for an updated price and address before ordering a book. If you can't find a book in your bookstore, you can usually get it directly from the publisher. Enclose $3 for shipping per book. You can order most titles from Amazon or other on-line book store. See page 208 for an order form for Morning Glory Press publications.

Biller, Henry B., and Trotter, Robert J. *The Father Factor: What You Need to Know to Make a Difference.* 1994. 243 pp. $10. Pocket Books. Note: This book is out of print but on-line book store may have limited quantities.
Explores the unique contributions that only a father can make in parenting. Gives the reader practical tools and advice to be the best father for his children.

Bjorklund, Barbara R. *Parents Book of Discipline.* 1999. 272 pp. $5.99. Mass Market Paperback.
Emphasizes that discipline is not the same as punishment, but is one of the fundamental ways that parents teach their children to respect others and themselves.

Blankenhorn, David. *Fatherless America: Confronting Our Most Urgent Social Problem.* 1996. 328 pp. $15. Harperperennial Library.
An important book promoting the importance of fathers, especially married fathers.

Brick, Peggy, et al. *The New Teaching Safer Sex.* 1998. $25. Center for Family Life Education, Planned Parenthood of Greater New Jersey. 973.539.9580 x120.
Advocates "safer sex" and provides lessons that actively involve students in learning how they can protect themselves.

Canfield, Ken R. *The 7 Secrets of Effective Fathers: Becoming the Father You Want to Be.* 1995. 244 pp. $10.99. Tyndale House Publishing, Wheaton, Illinois.
Offers research data from fathers across the country on the seven areas of expertise that Canfield says fathers need to acquire to become the best fathers they can be.

Clark, Ron. *Father Involvement: For Such a Time as This.* 2000. 29 pp. $6.50. For ordering information, call 757.865.4096 or contact <joyhouse1@gateway.net> 22 Bexley Lane, Hampton, VA 23666.
Emphasizes the importance of fathers in their children's lives. Also discusses how faith-based organizations as well as the church can become involved in strengthening father/child relationships.

Coles, Robert. *The Youngest Parents: Teenage Pregnancy as It Shapes Lives.* 2000. 224 pp. $19.99. W. W. Norton and Company, 800.233.4830.
An absorbing book which offers the compelling voices of young women and men, either pregnant or already parents, to provide yet another dimension to

*the realities of teen parents' lives. Includes nearly 100 pages of wonderful
black and white photos.*

Ekulona, Ademola. **The Healthy Start Father's Journal.** 1997.
Baltimore City Healthy Start, Inc., 210 Guilford Avenue, 2nd Floor,
Baltimore, MD 21202-3418. 410.396.7318.
*Afrocentric curriculum targeting inner-city males. Powerful chapters on
fatherhood, male-female relationships, anger management, and more.*

Fenwick, Elizabeth, and Richard Walker. **How Sex Works: A Clear,
Comprehensive Guide for Teenagers to Emotional, Physical, and
Sexual Maturity.** 1996. 96 pp. $9.95. DK Publishing, Inc.
212.213.4800.
*Profusely illustrated, easy-to-read comprehensive guide to emotional,
physical, and sexual maturity for teenagers.*

Gottfried, Ted. **Teen Fathers Today.** 2001. $23.90. Twenty First
Century Books.
*Focuses on teen fathers in America and their role in the childrearing
process. Real-life stories complement the discussions. Provides practical
information such as dealing with the reactions of parents, realities of
pregnancy and birth, and taking responsibility for one's baby.*

Green, Christopher. **Toddler Taming.** 1998. 288 pp. $11.95. Fawcett
Books.
*An excellent book written with humor. Good down to earth information for
parents of toddlers. Very readable.*

Harris, Robie H. Illus. by Michael Emberley. **It's Perfectly Normal:
Changing Bodies, Growing Up, Sex and Sexual Health.** 1996.
89 pp. $10.99. Candlewick Press.
*The illustrations are wonderful, and make it difficult to continue thinking of
sex as something we never talk about with our children.*

Horn, Wade F., Ph.D. **Father Facts.** Fourth Edition. 2002. 106 pp. $15.
The National Fatherhood Initiative, One Bank Street, Suite 160,
Gaithersburg, MD 20878. 301.948.0599.
*This book is filled with important facts, information, and research
concerning the plight of fatherlessness.*

_____, Alice Feinstein and Jeffery Rosenberg. **The New Father
Book: What Every Man Needs to Know to Be a Good Dad.** 1998.
96 pp. $9.95. Meredith Books.
*Gives fathers practical information and insight so they can become more
involved in their children's formative years.*

It Takes Two: For Teen Parents. 1997. 124 pp. Teachers Manual, $50; 26-page Student Manual, $6. Legacy Resource Group, P.O. Box 700, Carlisle, IA 50047. 515.989.3360.

It's a five-hour pregnancy prevention curriculum for teen parents. Encourages participants to look at their own values and their dreams, and to discuss how parenting has impacted those dreams. Emphasizes shared responsibility between men and women.

Jacobs, Thomas A., et al. *What Are My Rights? 95 Questions and Answers about Teens and the Law.* 1997. 208 pp. $14.95. Free Spirit Publishing. 612.338.2068.

A matter-of-fact guide to the laws that affect teens at home, at school, on the job, and in their communities.

Johnson, Jeffery, and Pamela Wilson. *Fatherhood Development: A Curriculum for Young Fathers.* 1994. 400 pp. $600 for curriculum and training. National Center for Strategic Nonprofit Planning and Community Leadership (NPCL), 2000 L Street NW, #815, Washington, DC 20036. 202.822.6725.

Excellent curriculum for teen father programs. Available only with training.

Lansky, Vicki. *101 Ways to Be a Special Dad.* 1993. 120 pp. $6.95. McGraw Hill.

Written as a Father's Day gift idea, this book contains tips for entertaining children — including taking a child to work for the day, reading the funnies together, planting a tree, and more.

Leach, Penelope. *Your Baby and Child from Birth to Age Five.* Revised, 1997. 560 pp. $20. Alfred A. Knopf. 800.733.3000.

An absolutely beautiful book packed with information, many color photos and lovely drawings. Comprehensive, authoritative, and outstandingly sensitive guide to child care and development.

Leving, Jeffery M., Kenneth A. Dachman, and Jeffrey Leving. *Fathers' Rights: Hard-hitting and Fair Advice for Every Father Involved in a Custody Dispute.* 1998. 240 pp. $15. Basic Books.

This powerful book provides accurate and authoritative information regarding child support and custody issues. Offers great insight for program providers.

Lindsay, Jeanne Warren. *The Challenge of Toddlers* and *Your Baby's First Year.* 1998. 224 pp. each. Paper, $12.95 each; hardcover, $18.95 each. Workbooks, $2.50 each. Morning Glory Press, 6595 San Haroldo Way, Buena Park, CA 90620. 888.612.8254.

How-to-parent books especially for teenage parents. Lots of quotes from teenage parents who share their experiences. Board games ($29.95 each), one for each of these titles, provide great learning reinforcement. Also see video series, Your Baby's First Year, described on page 204.

_____. *Do I Have a Daddy? A Story About a Single-Parent Child.* 2000. 48 pp. Paper, $7.95; hardcover, $14.95. Free study guide. Morning Glory Press.
A beautiful full-color picture book for the child who has never met his/her father. A special sixteen-page section offers suggestions to single mothers.

_____. *Teen Dads: Rights, Responsibilities and Joys.* 2001. 224 pp. $12.95. Complete curriculum, $95. Morning Glory Press.
Comprehensive parenting curriculum especially for teen dads. Includes lesson plans, handouts, and many activities.

_____. *Teen Parents and Their Parents: Managing Three-Generation Living When Mom or Dad Is a Teen.* 2003. 224 pp. $12.95. Morning Glory Press.
Can help the entire family adjust to their roles as an extended family.

_____. *Teenage Couples — Caring, Commitment and Change: How to Build a Relationship that Lasts. Teenage Couples — Coping with Reality: Dealing with Money, In-laws, Babies and Other Details of Daily Life.* 1995. 208, 192 pp. Paper, $9.95 ea.; hardcover, $15.95 ea. Workbooks and curriculum guide available. Morning Glory Press.
Series covers such important topics as communication, handling arguments, keeping romance alive, sex in a relationship, jealousy, alcohol and drug addiction, partner abuse, and divorce, as well as the practical details of living. Lots of quotes from teenage couples.

_____ and Jean Brunelli. *Nurturing Your Newborn: Young Parent's Guide to Baby's First Month.* 1999. 64 pp. $6.95. Morning Glory.
Adapted from chapters in Your Pregnancy and Newborn Journey and Your Baby's First Year which focus on the postpartum period. Ideal for teen parents home for a few weeks after delivery.

_____ and Sharon Enright. *Books, Babies and School-Age Parents: How to Help Pregnant and Parenting Teens Succeed.* 1997. 288 pp. Paper, $14.95; hardcover, $21.95. Morning Glory Press.
Help in understanding special issues of teenage parents and working more effectively with this special population.

_____ and Sally McCullough. *Discipline from Birth to Three.* 1998. 208 pp. Paper, $12.95; hardcover, $18.95. Morning Glory Press.

Provides teenage parents with guidelines to help prevent discipline problems with children and for dealing with problems when they occur.

McCoy, Kathy, et al. *The Teenage Body Book.* 1999. 288 pp. $18.95. Perigee Publishing.
Crammed with information for teenagers about everything from their bodies, changing feelings, and special medical needs of young adults to sexuality, sexually transmitted infections, birth control, pregnancy and parenthood. Lots of quotes from young people.

MELD Parenting Materials. Nueva Familia: Six books in Spanish and English. *Baby Is Here; Feeding Your Child, 5 months-2 years; Healthy Child, Sick Child; Safe Child and Emergencies; Baby Grows; Baby Plays.* 1992. $12 each. MELD, 123 North Third Street, Suite 507, Minneapolis, MN 55401. 612.332.7563.
Very easy to read booklets full of information. Designed especially for Mexican and Mexican American families, but excellent for anyone with limited reading skills. Ask MELD for catalog.

_____. *The New Middle of the Night Book: Answers to Young Parents' Questions When No One Is Around.* 1999. 163 pp. $12.50.
Includes clearly written information about parenting during the first two years of life. An especially good section discusses the benefits and how-tos of shared parenting, whether or not the parents are together as a couple.

Morris, Jon. *The For Males Only Curriculum.* 1997. 103 pp. $15. The Fatherhood and Families Program. 141 Campbell Avenue SW, Roanoke, VA 24011. <www.roadprogram.org>
Curriculum used by For Males Only staff for teen pregnancy prevention programs.

Nykiel, Connie. *What It Takes: A Survival Guide for Young and Teen Dads-to-Be.* 1999. 50 pp. $5. FemEd, 20670 Ashleaf Court, Sterling, VA 20165. 877.336.6338.
Booklet to help a teen father cope with his new life.

Parent Express Series: *Parent Express: For You and Your Infant; Spanish edition: Noticlas para los padres; Parent Express: For You and Your Toddler.* Each newsletter, 8 pp. $4 each set. ANR Publications, University of California, 6701 San Pablo Avenue, Oakland, CA 94608-1239. 510.642.2431.
Wonderful easy reading series of newsletters for parents. The first set, available in English and Spanish, starts two months before delivery and continues monthly through the first year of the child's life. Second set with twelve letters covers second and third years. Good resource for teen parents.

Parents as Teachers National Center, Inc. 10176 Corporate Square Drive, Ste. 230, St. Louis, MO 63132. 314.432.4330.
PAT is an early childhood parent education and family support program located in many communities throughout the United States. Their purpose is to empower all parents to give their child the best possible start in life. "Issues in Working with Teen Parents" is a specially designed training for professionals working with teen parents and their young children.

Parke, Ross D., and Armin A. Brott. **Throwaway Dads: The Myths and Barriers that Keep Men from Being the Fathers They Want to Be.** 1999. 252 pp. $3.99. Houghton Mifflin Company.
Amazing book that exposes the barriers and social biases that many fathers face when trying to become involved fathers.

Pollack, William. **Real Boys: Rescuing Our Sons from the Myths of Boyhood.** 1998. 447 pp. $15. Owl Books.
Groundbreaking research that explores why so many boys are sad, lonely, and confused, even though they appear tough and confident. Helps parents and teachers understand what boys are experiencing so we can help them become more nurturing and stable men.

Pollock, Sudie. **Will the Dollars Stretch? Teen Parents Living on Their Own.** 2001. 112 pp. $7.95. Teacher's Guide, $2.50. Morning Glory.
Five short stories about teen parents moving out on their own. (Two include the fathers.) As students read the stories, they will get the feel of poverty as experienced by many teen parents — as they write checks and balance the checkbooks of the young parents involved.

_____. **Moving On: Finding Information You Need for Living on Your Own.** 2001. 48 pp. $4.95. 25/$75. Morning Glory Press.
Fill-in guide to help young persons find information about their community, information needed for living away from parents.

Reynolds, Marilyn. **Too Soon for Jeff. True-to-Life Series from Hamilton High.** Novel. 1994. 224 pp. Paper, $8.95; hardcover, $15.95. Morning Glory Press.
Absorbing story of Jeff Browning, a senior at Hamilton High School, a nationally ranked debater, and reluctant father of Christy Calderon's unborn baby. Screen play based on the novel was an ABC After-School TV Special starring Freddie Prinze, Jr.

Seward, Angela. Illustrated by Donna Ferreiro. **Goodnight, Daddy.** 2001. 48 pp. Paper, $7.95; hardcover, $14.95. Morning Glory Press.
Beautiful full-color picture book — shows Phoebe's excitement because her father, who she hasn't seen in two years, is visiting her today. She is

devastated when he calls to say "Something has come up." Book illustrates the importance of father in the life of his child.

Silberg, Jackie. *125 Brain Games for Babies.* 1999. 143 pp. $14.95. Consortium Book Sales.
Packed with everyday games, songs, and other opportunities to continue the brain development of children from birth through twelve months. Illustrated.

Sonenstein, Freya L., Kellie Stewart, Laura Duberstein Lindberg, Marta Pernas, and Sean Williams. *Involving Males in Preventing Teen Pregnancy.* 1997. 176 pp. $10. The Urban Institute. 2100 M Street NW, Washington, D.C. 20037. <www.urban.org>
Fantastic guide for program planners wanting to start or enhance their teen pregnancy prevention program. Highlights several successful male focused programs.

Stewart, Nancy. *Your Baby from Birth to 18 Months: The Complete Illustrated Guide.* 1997. 192 pp. $15.95. Fisher Books.
Provides clear and valid information about caring for the new baby on up to age 18 months. Well illustrated.

Turner, Randell D., and Martha C. Eichenlaub. *Long Distance Dads.* 1998. 238 page curriculum. $350. With training, $475. National Fatherhood Initiative.
Curriculum for fathers who are incarcerated.

Watnik, Webster. *Child Custody Made Simple: Understanding the Laws of Child Custody and Child Support.* 1999. 457 pp. $21.95. Single Parent Press, P.O. Box 1298, Claremont, CA 91711.
Easy to read book that will answer the many questions about child custody and child support whether you are separated, divorced, or never married.

Weinberg, Pamela. *Your Home Is a Learning Place.* 1995. 64 pp. $9.75. New Readers Press.
Contains simple activities and strategies that can help parents enhance their child's learning, often in the context of things parents already do.

Wise Guys: Male Responsibility. 1995. 250 pp. $150 + shpg. *Wise Guys: The Next Level.* 2000. 250 pp. $150. Family Life Council of Greater Greensboro, Inc., 310 East Washington Street, Suite 204, Greensboro, NC 27401.
Male Responsibility is a male focused curriculum for use with boys ages 10-15. The Next Level is curriculum for high school and college age men. Includes a fatherhood component. Training is available and recommended.

VIDEOS — Sources, Representative Titles
(Contact distributors for current listings.)

Baby Basics. 1989. 110 min. $24.95. Karol Video, P.O. Box 7600, Wilkes-Barre, PA 18773. 800.526.4773.
Provides instruction, demonstration, and support to new and expectant parents. The tape highlights four families of different races and socio-economic backgrounds interacting with their infants. Easily shown in sections. Lots of information.

Breastfeeding and Basketball. 1999. 8 min. $79.95. Injoy Videos, 1435 Yarmouth Avenue, Suite 102-D, Boulder, CO 80304. 800.326.2082.
A partner's support is a great help for a breastfeeding mother. Four men, while playing basketball, talk about advantages of breastfeeding. They're not teenagers, but teens can enjoy and learn from this light-hearted video.

The Dad Film. 1989. 28 min. $39.95. Injoy Videos.
Four new fathers share their personal experiences of fatherhood. Intimately and humorously they address the question, "What's it really going to be like to be a dad?"

Discipline from Birth to Three. Four videos, **Infants and Discipline —Meeting Baby's Needs, He's Crawling — Help!** (6-12 months), **She's into Everything!** (1-2 years), and **Your Busy Runabout** (2-3 years). 2001. 15 min. each. $195 set, $69.95 each. Morning Glory Press, 6595 San Haroldo Way, Buena Park, CA 90620. 888.612.8254.
Wonderful videos over book of same title. Shows teens talking to teens, sharing techniques for loving care. Teaching guide includes discussion questions, writing and research assignments, and quiz.

Exercise with Daddy and Me. 1996. 50 min. $39.95. Injoy Videos.
Shows a class with a pediatrician, who is also a dad, as he helps fathers and babies bond through movement, music, and massage.

Getting Men Involved. Three-video series. 2001. 15-35 min. Prices below. KidSafety of America, 6251 Schaefer Ave., Suite B, Chino, CA 91710, 909.902.1340.
One focuses on the importance of men getting involved in childcare, education, and social work (15 min. $79.95). Another video focuses on young men as fathers, produced for educators and caregivers, and includes suggestions on implementing and maintaining a fatherhood program (35 min. $79.95). The third video is for teens and other young fathers (15 min., $59.95).

Fatherhood USA. Three tapes: **Dedicated Not Deadbeat, Juggling Family and Work,** and **Workshop and Workbook.** 2000. Each tape, $34.95 ppd. for individuals; $114 ppd. for institutions. Three tapes and workbook, $74.95 and $250. Media Library, 22 Hollywood Avenue, Ho Ho Kus, NJ 07423. 800.343.5540.
PBS series on fatherhood hosted by former Senator Bill Bradley. Shows young fathers, teens and early 20s, in fatherhood groups. Realistic, good.

Infant and Toddler First Aid: Accidents (Vol. 1), Illnesses (Vol. 2). 1994. 36, 43 min. Both, $49.95. Injoy Videos.
Volume 1 teaches parents about the most common childhood accidents and includes easy-to-follow instructions on what to do until help arrives. Volume 2 explains what to do when a child becomes ill or is in danger from poisoning, fever, seizure, choking and more. Includes a clear demonstration of CPR, and has a segment on creating a home first-aid kit.

Jenny's Birth. 1993. 13 min. $90. Injoy Videos.
Jenny and Ernesto, a teen Hispanic couple, struggle with a long, difficult labor to deliver a healthy 6-pound son by cesarean section.

Shaking, Hitting, Spanking . . . What to Do Instead. 1990. 1995. Spanish. 30 min. $89.95. Injoy Videos.
Shows easy-to-use techniques of discipline with four common scenes that often lead to shaking, hitting, or spanking a child. After each scene, you can stop the video and brainstorm alternative behaviors. The video then presents a number of proven, common-sense, parenting techniques.

Teen Dads. 18 min. $95. United Learning, 1560 Sherman Avenue, #100, Evanston, IL 60201. 800.421.2363.
Four teen fathers who have chosen to play an active role in their children's lives are profiled in this video about responsibility, hard decisions, and planning ahead.

Too Soon for Jeff. 1996. 40 min. $89.95. Films for the Humanities and Sciences, P.O. Box 2053, Princeton, NJ 08543. 800.257.5126.
ABC After-School TV Special was based on the award-winning novel by Marilyn Reynolds. Starring Freddie Prinze, Jr., it's an excellent adaptation of novel about reluctant teen father.

Your Baby's First Year. 1996, 2001. Four videos. **Nurturing Your Newborn, She's Much More Active** (4-8 months), **Leaving Baby Stage Behind, Keeping Baby Healthy.** $195 set; $69.95 each. Morning Glory Press.
Teens talking to teens, sharing techniques for loving care. Based on book, with same title. Includes teacher's guide with questions, projects, quiz.

INDEX

About the Author

Jon Morris has provided services and programs to young men for more than seven years. Upon graduation in 1994 from Ferrum College, Ferrum, VA, Jon began his career at the Baptist Children's Home in Salem, VA, as a counselor in their Emergency Care Division for boys aged 8-18. In 1995, Jon became the first full-time coordinator of the For Males Only program for the Roanoke City Health Department, Roanoke, VA.

Jon is the co-founder of the Reaching Out to Adolescent Dads program, and also serves as the chairperson and founder of the Roanoke Valley Fatherhood Coalition.

In July, 2001, Jon, his staff, and the For Males Only program moved from the Health Department to Total Action Against Poverty (TAP). Jon currently serves as program manager for the Fatherhood and Families program at TAP, which holds the For Males Only, Reaching Out to Adolescent Dads (ROAD), and the Fathers at Work programs.

Jon has served as a consultant to the Virginia Fatherhood Campaign and regularly speaks on fatherhood issues throughout the Commonwealth of Virginia. In addition, he has provided valuable information to many programs across the country concerning fatherhood and male-targeted programming.

Jon lives in Roanoke, VA, with his wife, Katrina, and their two children, Ameer and Nina.

Photographer for ***ROAD to Fatherhood***, J. O. Claytor, has received many awards for community service.

ORDER FORM

Morning Glory Press
6595 San Haroldo Way, Buena Park, CA 90620
714.828.1998; 888.612.8254 Fax 714.828.2049

			Price	Total
___	*ROAD to Fatherhood* 1-885356-92-7		$14.95	_____
___	Hardcover 1-885356-91-9		21.95	_____
	Teen Dads: Rights, Responsibilities and Joys			
___	Book only — 1-885356-68-4		12.95	_____
___	*Teen Dads Comprehensive Curriculum*		95.00	_____
___	*Books, Babies and School-Age Parents*			
	1-885356-22-6		14.95	_____
	Your Pregnancy and Newborn Journey			
___	1-885356-30-7		12.95	_____
___	*Your Baby's First Year* 1-885356-33-1		12.95	_____
___	*The Challenge of Toddlers* 1-885356-39-0		12.95	_____
___	*Discipline from Birth to Three* 1-885356-36-6		12.95	_____
___	*Breaking Free from Partner Abuse*			
___	1-885356-53-6		8.95	_____
___	*Teen Parents and Their Parents* 1-885356-94-3		12.95	_____
___	*Safer Sex: The New Morality* 1-885356-66-8		14.95	_____
	Teen Moms: Pain, Promise 1-885356-25-0		14.95	_____
	Teenage Couples: Expectations and Reality			
___	0-930934-98-9		14.95	_____
	— Caring, Commitment and Change			
___	0-930934-93-8		9.95	_____
	— Coping with Reality 0-930934-86-5		9.95	_____
___	*Will the Dollars Stretch?* 1-885356-78-1		7.95	_____
___	*Moving On* 1-885356-81-1		4.95	_____
Novels by Marilyn Reynolds:				
___	*Love Rules*	1-885356-76-5	9.95	_____
___	*If You Loved Me*	1-885356-55-2	8.95	_____
___	*Baby Help*	1-885356-27-7	8.95	_____
___	*But What About Me?*	1-885356-10-2	8.95	_____
___	*Too Soon for Jeff*	0-930934-91-1	8.95	_____
___	*Detour for Emmy*	0-930934-76-8	8.95	_____
___	*Telling*	1-885356-03-x	8.95	_____
___	*Beyond Dreams*	1-885356-00-5	8.95	_____

TOTAL _____

Add postage: 10% of total—Min., $3.50; 15%, Canada _____
California residents add 7.75% sales tax _____

TOTAL _____

Ask about quantity discounts, teacher, student guides.
Prepayment requested. School/library purchase orders accepted.
If not satisfied, return in 15 days for refund.

NAME _____

PHONE_____ Purchase Order #_____

ADDRESS _____

_____